Marriage on the Mend
Tangible Tools to Restore Your Relationship

Clint and Penny A. Bragg

Marriage on the Mend—
Tangible Tools to Restore Your Relationship
Clint and Penny A. Bragg

Printed in the United States of America
Copyright ©2008 by Clint and Penny Bragg, Port Orange, FL
Second printing, 2009. Golden Gate Litho, Oakland, CA.
Library of Congress Catalog Number TXu 1-600-879

Cover Design: Angelina Gonzales, NThreeQ Media, www.nthreeq.com
Cover Photographs: P.A. Bragg
Back Cover Biography Photograph: Greg Schneider,
www.gregschneider.com

Scripture taken from the HOLY BIBLE, NEW INTERNATIONAL
VERSION®. Copyright © 1973, 1978, 1984 by International Bible
Society. Used by permission of Zondervan. All rights reserved.

NIV and *NEW INTERNATIONAL VERSION* are trademarks registered
in the United States Patent and Trademark Office by the International
Bible Society.

Inverse Ministries, Inc.
www.inverseministries.org
www.marriageonthemend.com

ISBN 978-0-9765661-6-8

"...to Jesus the mediator of a new covenant, and to the sprinkled blood that speaks a better word."

Hebrews 12:24

Marriage on the Mend
Tangible Tools to Restore Your Relationship

Clint and Penny A. Bragg

Table of Contents

Marriage on the Mend Workbook

The *Marriage on the Mend* workbook serves as a study companion for this book and is designed for couples or small groups. Each of the twelve lessons in the workbook builds upon the concepts, ideas, and tools shared in *Marriage on the Mend*. Small group interaction is facilitated through strategies such as discussion vignettes, Scripture reading, lesson principles, and applicable activities. In addition, the workbook is designed to help couples…

- Identify reconciliation roadblocks
- Draft a set of biblically-based marriage standards
- Effectively handle painful experiences from the past
- Integrate prayer and Bible study into their relationship
- Understand the importance of accountability
- Set and assess goals related to their relationship
- Implement tools that will deepen intimacy
- Proactively safeguard their marriage

Order your copy today!
www.inverseministries.org
www.marriageonthemend.com

A Letter from the Authors

On the wall of our office, there's a large map. Using color-coded *Post-it*™ notes, we use this map to track and pray for couples in crisis across the nation and abroad. Each time we receive a call or an e-mail, we identify the city, state, and country of the person contacting us and the current status of his/her marriage. A purple *Post-it* note means the couple is in crisis, but still living under the same roof. Bright pink means they've separated, and blue indicates their divorce has been finalized. One glance at our prayer map is proof positive that Satan is serving up marriage and family on a skewer and it's tearing our world in two.

One of the most distressing aspects of our work is that, each day, we see the widespread havoc divorce is wreaking across all racial, educational, socio-economic, and denominational boundaries. Just today we received word that a bitter custody battle in a nearby state ended when a father murdered his three children to get back at his wife.[1]

Before working with troubled marriages, we served as educators in the public school system. Each day we witnessed the fall-out of marital dysfunction on the faces of our students. Within the first few days of school it was easy to tell which students were living in healthy homes and which students weren't. How can a teacher justify getting all worked up at a fourth grader for not completing her homework when her mother called the police on her father the night before?

The bottom line is this: There's a war raging and we're rising up against the wrong opponent. Spouses are doing battle with each another and their children instead of fighting the real Enemy.

No matter what tragedies have transpired in your marriage, your spouse is not the culprit. Allow us to give you just one example of how rising up against the wrong enemy is playing out in thousands of marriages at this very moment.

A husband who has been hiding his addiction to pornography is finally caught in the act by his wife. Her discovery brings an onslaught of rage. "How could you do this to me? To our family?" Her head is spinning. Distraught, she storms out of the house and formulates a plan to leave her husband. In the back of her mind, she's already decided that divorce is her *only* option. In a single moment, her whole world has been turned upside down. She's reeling and it's all *his* fault. "I'll never forgive him for this!" Disgusted, hurt, and betrayed, she rises up against her husband.

For years, he feared his wife would discover his secret. Now...she knows. Shame sickens his gut. Spinning through his mind are all the things he stands to lose. "What have I done?" Unworthiness overtakes him and he begins to sob. He has resolved to stop surfing the Internet thousands of times, but he just can't seem to quit. "What's wrong with me?" Confused and repulsed by the man he's become, he rises up against himself.

Maybe this scenario hits close to home. Or, perhaps it wasn't an addiction that tore your marriage in two, but a person. Over the years, we've received numerous e-mails from spouses whose mates left them for someone else. Fidelity was never intended to be a fantasy or some lofty ideal but sadly, mutual faithfulness in marriage has become something of a rare breed. Some of these individuals told us their spouses abandoned the marriage for a same-sex relationship and the pain from *that* sort of betrayal was more than they could bear. For others, a series of problems and chronic arguing had finally taken their toll.

No matter what the intimate details involve, every person who contacts us feels as though they've been cut to the core. Based on their experiences as well as our own, we've come to realize that there's one thing all these different scenarios have in common. Whether it's family drama, debt, addiction, infidelity, or rebellion, the manifestation of marital breakdown is a secondary issue of something far greater: an unmet need for true intimacy and unconditional love that's been lodged in our DNA since the Fall.

Let's be honest. At one level or another, every one of us is guilty of trying to fill legitimate needs with counterfeit means. It's the Enemy's most underhanded weapon and it's tearing at the fabric of our very existence. Our intent in writing this letter is not to split theological or psychological hairs over why we do the things we do. There are counselors, professors, pastors, and scholars whose years of study and research can speak to these things far better than we ever could. Instead, the intent in putting our convictions on these pages is to set the stage for a sobering question that is the underlying premise for this entire book:

What if?

What if the wife described earlier was to rise up against the real Enemy instead of her husband? What if her husband stopped condemning himself or anyone else for his problems and instead, placed blame where blame belonged? And, what if both parties—broken and humbled before God—confessed their individual part in the breakdown of the marriage, received His forgiveness, and extended forgiveness to one another?

What if you and your spouse did the very same thing?

Listen. We're not saying that sinful behavior should be shrugged off or glossed over. Nothing could be further from the truth. Sin is sin and it must be dealt with. Those of us who've inappropriately indulged in self-gratification at *any* level must deal with the consequences of our actions. What we are saying is that all outward manifestations of marital division have, as their source, a wound that runs much deeper. And, historically, it is an ache that has been gravely misunderstood. Until the true source of that ache is unveiled and addressed, the heights of intimacy and restoration in your marriage will fall far short of what God intends.

What is this great ache gnawing at our hearts? Proverbs 19:22 says it best: *"What a man desires is unfailing love."* Much

14

of the rest of the Bible contains undeniable proof that human beings are capable of doing just about anything to be loved. We were, too.

Relationships, material possessions, sex, academic pursuits, career achievements, food—you name it. Between the two of us, we tried many remedies in search of that one thing that would soothe our souls' ache. And, we're pleased to report that all of our attempts to find love failed...except for one.

Years of pining after lesser lovers resulted in the discovery that *nothing* on earth was created to fill the great void in our hearts. We were created with a God-sized gap and, try as we might, nothing can ever take His rightful place.

There's one more colored *Post-it* note on our marriage prayer map. A yellow note indicates that a couple has chosen to begin the process of restoring their marriage. Placing a yellow *Post-it* on the map brings us to our knees in humble gratitude for it symbolizes yet another couple who has decided to answer the highest call imaginable: the call to forgive.

Division has inhabited far too great a territory. Battles between spouses are littering the landscape on every continent, leaving children in their wake. We look upon the devastation and the way in which it impacts this generation—as well as the threat it poses for the next—and our hearts break.

God's heart is breaking, too.

So, in light of this truth, we must ask you today: *What if?* God has the desire to completely restore your marriage. What if you allow Him to do the very thing for which His heart longs?

It was one letter, written years ago, that started the restoration process in our marriage. It is our earnest prayer that the letter you are now reading will do the same for you. We resolutely believe that the once-threatening tide of divorce will dramatically turn when we rise from the ruins...and forgive.

Rising with you,
Clint and Penny Bragg

We were married just over two years when we came to the realization that we really didn't know how to function together as a marital team. If God hadn't interceded and stirred within our hearts to totally change us back then, we're certain that we would not be married today. We were two selfish individuals who thought we knew it all. It wasn't until we got on our knees together and asked God to teach us how to make our marriage work, that we started heading in a healthy direction. God put hope in our hearts that, in time, things would get better. And, they did.

There are times when we wish we could tell other couples that there is a "quick fix" to their marriage problems, but we haven't seen it be so. Oftentimes, a quick fix only means a temporary one. What we've discovered is that as marriage partners, we must partner with God to address each other's needs and participate in His process of healing.

The restoration of our marriage is a work that continues to this day as God reveals the different aspects of our selfishness that need to be broken and made into the image of what He would have for our lives together. The process has taken intentionality and a proactive mindset to get our marriage to a place where it reflects the heart of Christ.

God has a plan for every person (individually and corporately) in their married lives and it should be their mission to find out what it is and how they can help each other get there.

Steve and Cindy Wright
Founders of *Marriage Missions International*
Tucson, AZ

Chapter 1 – Honoring the Process

Every broken marriage has the hope of becoming a saved marriage. Why? Because there is *no* marriage in such a state of ruin that it remains beyond God's reach. In our ministry to couples in crisis across the nation, we often conclude our testimony by sharing this one truth: "If God can reconcile *our* marriage, He can reconcile any relationship." This is our message to you as well.

We are living proof that, against all odds, God can mend a marriage. Originally married to each other on September 2, 1989, we sailed through our first year together without incident. But, by our second year of marriage, irritations and differences that were once fairly benign began to create a steady stream of conflict. Our prayers for a permanent solution—or at least a quick-fix—remained unanswered. Before long, we couldn't agree on anything, including the source of our discontent. Something was definitely broken and, try as we might, we just couldn't fix it. To complicate matters, we were too proud to tell anyone that our relationship was on the rocks. As a result, the emotional, physical, and spiritual breach between us only widened.

The fragile state of our marriage created the perfect scenario for me (Penny) to start looking elsewhere for comfort. Clint confronted me about his suspicions regarding an affair, but I vehemently denied his accusations. The tension between us mounted until one balmy evening just prior to our second anniversary, I packed a few things in a suitcase and rolled it out the door. The last time we saw each other was the day our divorce papers were notarized, citing: "Irreconcilable differences have caused the permanent breakdown of our marriage."

Fast forward eleven years, 3,000 coast-to-coast miles, and a series of divinely orchestrated events, and God miraculously reconciled our marriage. On August 17, 2002, we were married again in front of all of our family and friends. Throughout the remainder of this book, we'll share more of our story. But, what's important for you to know right now is that even though God reconciled our marriage, we incorrectly assumed the hard part was behind us. Shortly after saying, "I do," for the second time, we discovered that nothing could be further from the truth.

This is just one of the unique scenarios couples initially face after deciding they want to make their marriages work. Depending upon the history of the relationship, other complications also enter in and cloud the mix such as past betrayal, financial deficits, lack of intimacy, unsupportive opinions from others, and more. Learning to love the same person anew begins to feel daunting and attempts to toss in the towel can unexpectedly resurface.

We'll be straight-up with you. Marriage is messy. Reconciling a relationship after a crisis, separation, divorce, or all of the above is even messier. You will face problems—old and new ones—along the way. But, you are not alone. We had our fair share of troubles too, just like every other couple we've served in ministry. Many times, people will tell us that the problems contributing to the fragmentation of their marriages are far too ugly for repairs to ever be made. They aren't ready to get real with God or each other. As a result, they seriously doubt their relationship can be mended. Simply stated, that's a cop-out. If you sincerely want to get well, and you want your marriage to get well, then you're already on the road to wholeness and healing.

19

Depending upon your marriage history, the rebuilding process may seem complicated right now. That's normal. Make no mistake; the restoration of a marriage is both incredibly euphoric and agonizingly painful. Expect the process to take time and hard work. Unfortunately, it's much easier to fight than to forgive.

There were many times when we honestly disclosed our mistakes before God and each other...and wept over the consequences of our sins and shortcomings. During those times, we wanted nothing more than to cover our heads, tuck our respective tails between our legs, and walk away from each other in sulking defeat. However, we can also say that engaging in the hard work of re-establishing our marriage covenant with God and one another has been unlike anything we ever thought was within the realm of possibility. The shedding of Christ's blood— combined with our own sweat and tears—has resulted in wholeness and healing that is incomparable in worth or measure. The same can be said for your marriage as well. Your restoration begins with answering "yes" to the two questions we ask the couples who contact us for help: Are you at the bottom of the bottom? And, do you want to get well?

Would Our Marriage Make it the Second Time Around?

According to a March, 2008 survey conducted by *The Barna Group*, "Among those who have said their wedding vows, one out of three have been divorced at least once."[2] Overall, national divorce rates are said to be on the rise, but statistics are sketchy, at best, regarding the percentage of couples who successfully reconcile after a crisis or separation, or those who, like us, remarry their former spouses. It's safe to assume, however, that couples who reconcile definitely do not have the odds of success stacked in their favor. Neither did we.

"Our marriage has to make it this time!" I (Penny) cried as we stood arguing in the kitchen shortly after we remarried. Our honeymoon high lasted about as long as our wedding day. Once the reception was over and the guests had gone, we hit conflict. When all was said and done, the source of our disagreement paled in comparison to the stark realization that our marriage would fail again if we didn't get some help. We loved each other and we loved God, but our first marriage to each other proved that those things simply weren't enough.

"Are you going to leave me again?" Clint asked with tears rolling down his cheeks. The honesty and vulnerability of his question all but bowled me over backwards. Of course I wasn't going to leave him again, but that first disagreement after remarrying triggered some painful memories of previous conflicts in our first marriage and neither one of us knew what to do about it. It took days to sort through the clutter, expose our true feelings, and acknowledge our fears.

"There has to be another way to do this," I sobbed as we sat down to sort things out several nights later. As Clint and I discussed what led up to our disagreement, we realized God had captured our full attention during that stand-off. The source of our conflict centered on something rather trivial, but it wasn't the magnitude of it that mattered. The real problem was that we had no proactive plan to resolve conflict—large or small—inevitable in every normal marriage. What made matters even more challenging was that our marriage was far from any norm we'd ever known.

We'd never heard of anyone whose marriage was successfully mended after spending as many years apart as we had. In vain, we began to search for resources that specifically spoke to the unique challenges of restoring a broken marriage. It

21

was our very desperate search that, years down the road, led us to write this book. What you are now holding is the culmination of everything we learned about restoring our relationship during the first five years of our remarriage. To this day, every tangible tool we share is faithfully practiced in our marriage and each one has been designed to help couples navigate through the troubled waters that accompany their decisions to reconcile.

True Restoration Takes Time

In our current work as full-time marriage missionaries, we travel across the nation on *40-Day Marriage Mission Trips,* sharing our testimony of reconciliation and assisting couples who have lost all hope. Not only have we experienced the full restoration of our own relationship with these tools, but we've also witnessed countless other couples who've overcome the odds by using them.

While we realize that our testimony is quite extraordinary, we share only a small portion of it with you in this chapter in order to emphasize this important fact: true restoration takes time and you must honor the process. Eleven years may seem a bit extreme, but our story illustrates that God's processes and timelines are just as important, if not more so, than the final outcome. During our years apart, there were major overhauls that needed to happen in our individual hearts. After we finally remarried, we had yet another long road ahead.

Speaking from our experience and those of the other people to whom we've ministered, once a couple decides they want to work things out, there is a sense of urgency to immediately "fix" all the problems from the past. However, you must be willing to respect *whatever* timelines God uses to heal your relationship and to entrust the entire process to Him. Consider this: it probably took awhile for your marriage to get to the point of crisis, separation, and/or divorce. Typically, troubles in a marriage don't surface overnight. More than likely, there was a compounding nature to your circumstances, conflicts, and differences that mounted over time. Left unresolved, these things created division. With enough compounding fractures and no effective intervention, a divided marriage can't help but fail. That being the case, it's going to take time for the relationship to heal. No matter what your situation is today, if you accept the fact that it will take ample time to get the relationship properly realigned and back out onto the road, you'll make significant progress at an early stage.

Perhaps you and your spouse experienced such repeated discord that you separated. Some of you may have even gone as far as divorce, like we did. There is hope! Even what you may consider to be the darkest detours of your relationship (i.e., infidelity, addiction, abuse, bankruptcy, etc.) can be completely transformed when you're both willing to submit your timelines to God. If you truly want to get well, God will do His part as you do yours.

Once we realized it was going to take some time to restore our relationship, we made a very important agreement we'd like you to consider. During our first year back together, we consciously made the restoration of our marriage our top priority (second only to our individual relationships with God). We wanted God to know that we were serious about devoting quality time to our marriage in order to heal. Being intentional about our relationship wasn't something we'd done the first time around.

In addition, because we both possessed a tendency to have over-committed schedules, this agreement ensured that we were not running ahead of God. In order to intentionally invest in our restoration during that first year, we agreed not to take on any new responsibilities or endeavors. Promotions, projects, or

23

leadership opportunities—no matter how exciting or noble—were simply turned down or put on hold. This agreement also included not accepting offers to serve in any *ongoing* roles at our church. Does that sound selfish? *Hear us out.* We struggled with the idea too, at first. But, we knew that if we didn't get intentional about mending our marriage, we would be of no service to our church or to God.

So, instead of trying to balance a bunch of new responsibilities, we attended church each week, worshipped God side-by-side, listened attentively to our pastor's sermons, and talked to couples we could trust. If there were marriage conferences or workshops we knew we'd benefit from, we attended those as well. We also committed to reading and discussing several Christian books together during that first year and learning as much as we could from other married couples. Prioritizing the time needed to restore our marriage gave us the chance to be more intentional with each other.

These commitments had a profound impact on our restoration. In hindsight, we realize we could have helped our cause more had we taken the time to clearly explain these priorities to our pastors, family members, bosses, close friends, and colleagues. That way, they would have understood the importance we were placing on our marriage this time around. So please, learn from our mistakes. We highly recommend that you communicate your priorities to the people who most closely surround you. You will find that proactively communicating the emphasis you're placing on your marriage strengthens your support system and alleviates misunderstandings as to the reasons behind the choices you are making.

During the coming months, you'll need guidance as you reassess, regroup, and prayerfully rebuild your relationship. There are many ideas in this book that will help you gain and maintain perspective. Although the drama of marital conflict may differ drastically from one couple to the next, the time and tools it takes to mend these marriages are very similar.

Woven throughout the tapestry of this text is sound advice from couples who have done (and continue to do) the hard work of restoring their marriages, as well as applicable bits and pieces from our own experiences. While each couple featured is unique, they also all have several things in common. Most importantly, they know that *God* saved their marriages. In addition, they all made it through the fire of their crisis and came out on the other side far more relationally wealthy than when they went in. Finally, each couple grew more intimate with God and, as a result, with each other.

While all these couples share similarities, we also want to convey that every marriage survival story is unique depending upon the nature of the crisis (or crises) that contributed to its breakdown. While we include the experiences of many couples in this book, please understand that the ways in which God restores one relationship may not be exactly the same way He restores another.

Learning from the Past

Even though this book includes portions of our story and those of other couples, none of these examples should take precedence over the truths in God's Word. In light of that, written accounts from the experiences of the prophet, Nehemiah, are threaded throughout almost every chapter of *Marriage on the Mend*. Although the book of Nehemiah, where the prophet's task of rebuilding the war-torn walls around Jerusalem is recorded, was not specifically written about marriage, it is a perfect biblical parallel for restoring your relationship.

To properly set the scene, understand that at the opening of Nehemiah, a representative remnant of the Israelite nation had just returned to Jerusalem after seventy years of Babylonian exile. During that time, God sent prophets to restore the community. Their work included rebuilding the massive wall surrounding the city. Enter Nehemiah. Against fierce opposition, social and economic devastation, threats of attack, chronic sin, and evildoers who repeatedly attempted to stop him, we'll see how this persevering prophet succeeded in completing what God had called him to accomplish.

There are no set rules as to the pace of proceeding through this book and the tangible tools we share. Again, one thing all broken relationships have in common is that true healing takes time. Resist the temptation to skip over implementing the tools or rushing through the pages of *Marriage on the Mend*. Instead, we encourage you to take the time to complete all the exercises and answer the questions at the end of each chapter because they are designed to help your relationship become more resilient. We also advise you to repeat any of these exercises as time passes and your relationship changes. Trust the advice in this book the way you would a wise mentor. We'd like nothing more than to walk beside you through each page. It is a humble privilege to use our past for your future.

Before you continue to read on, take time to pray. Ask God to help you get the most from what we've written. Ask Him to help you learn from your past, as well as from ours and the other couples you'll meet through the pages of this book. Let Him know you're willing to be participants in this process. Acknowledge that He is in total control of both your ruins and your restoration. Remember, what's happening in your marriage right now is far greater than just the two of you. Your children, extended family, and friends are significantly affected by your marriage. Never minimize the magnitude of what you are about to begin. Restoring your relationship will undoubtedly impact the current generation as well as generations to come. The reconciliation of one marriage under God possesses the power to change families and nations throughout the world, alter the course of human history, and ultimately…increase the population of heaven! That's what matters most.

In order to effectively maneuver around the roadblocks you'll encounter together, make a conscious and irrevocable decision to choose reconciliation each day for the rest of your lives, especially amidst trials and turbulent waters that occur as a natural part of mending your marriage. In the next chapter, we'll help you recognize the specific roadblocks that may be threatening to impede your progress before you even get started.

CHAPTER EXERCISES

Prayer for the Process of Restoration

Teach us, Father, to rest all our demands and desires for the restoration of this relationship in Your hands. Transform them into the desire to be strong and steadfast in You. When we are weak, You are strong and You receive the glory. Be the Lord of what's left of our time together. We relinquish all of our hours and expectations for this marriage to You. Help us not to hoard time in order to serve our private agendas. We cannot condemn anyone, including ourselves, for the time we've lost, and we let go of the time yet before us. We place You in charge of our ruins and their restoration. And, we let go of hurriedness to truly experience Your healing. We want to get well, God. Heal us. In Jesus' name. Amen.

Make a Timeline

Create a timeline of your marriage that spans the last five years. If you haven't been married very long, modify the timeline to better fit your needs. (Option: you may even want to start your timeline on your wedding day and work forward from there. The choice is yours.)

Begin by drawing a horizontal line across a large piece of butcher paper. Above the line, list the major physical, emotional, financial, logistical, and spiritual life events that have *positively* impacted your relationship. Below the line, list the major physical, emotional, financial, logistical, and spiritual life events that have *negatively* impacted your relationship.

It's normal for spouses to differ regarding what each one considers to be a positive or negative life event. As a result, the same event may be listed in both the upper and lower section of the timeline. For example, a husband may feel that his job promotion was a positive life event while his wife feels his promotion was negative because he was away on business all the time and she was left alone to care for the children without his help.

Completing this project will take more than one sitting as you think about all of the life events in your marriage history. As you remember more details, add them to the timeline. This timeline will serve as an insightful way to trace some of your current conflicts back to their original sources.

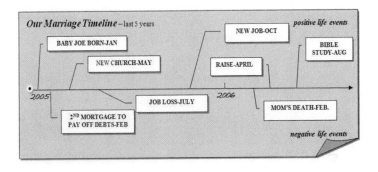

Scripture Reading

Read Nehemiah 1 before answering the questions on the next page.

Questions to Consider

1. What did you notice about your relationship after reviewing the major life events on the timeline?

2. While creating the timeline, were you in agreement as to what you viewed as positive and negative? Why or why not?

3. What else did you notice as you looked back over the events/years?

4. Can you see how events or changes might have led up to a crisis in your relationship?

5. What did you notice about Nehemiah's approach to rebuilding the wall of Jerusalem? How did he set out to deal with the restoration process and how does this relate to your marriage?

Scott and Cathy were married on August 3, 1991. By the second year of their marriage, they had both accepted Christ and become involved in a local church. However, having God in their lives was no guarantee that their marriage was going to make it. At the apex of their crisis, they'd been married just over eleven years and had three small children; ages six, four, and two. Solely for the sake of the kids, Scott and Cathy never physically separated, but they were living separate lives under the same roof for many months before finally letting down their defenses.

"Once we finally decided we wanted to make our marriage work, the first thing we *both* did was to take personal responsibility for our own actions. We had to intentionally take our eyes off each other and start changing the things that we could change in our individual hearts. There was to be no more blaming or pointing fingers. It was time for both of us to own up to our part of the problem and to let God make the *first* changes there."

Scott and Cathy Jones
Winshape Retreat Center
Rome, GA

Chapter 2 – Recognizing Your Roadblocks

Imagine that you and your spouse have decided to venture out for a long drive. You've taken the day off work, packed the car, and precisely mapped out your adventure. Everything is running smoothly, at first. After driving for several hours, however, you come across an unexpected roadblock in the highway and are forced to stop the car. At this point you have an important decision to make and there are several options to consider.

You could heed the sign, turn the car around, and find another way to get to your destination. Or, you might choose to go someplace else. Another possibility might be to turn off the engine, wait for another car to approach the roadblock, follow their lead, and see how it all turns out for them. Perhaps you would take a more risky approach: ignore the roadblock, move it out of the way, and continue down the road, regardless of the consequences.

Your decision regarding this roadblock hinges on many contributing factors. Is there really something dangerous up ahead? If so, how dangerous is it? Are you afraid? Was the roadblock erected to protect you? Or, was it put there as a detour? Are there past experiences, emotions, or other issues contributing to your decision? Have you ever faced this roadblock before? If so, what did you do and what was the outcome? What does your spouse think you should do? Do you agree with him/her? What impact is this one choice going to have on your plans? On your marriage? On your children?

We use this example to demonstrate what often occurs when couples reconcile and come face-to-face with their first challenge. It's not just the roadblock that must be considered. Depending upon a couple's history, there are many other things that factor into the scenario and complicate matters. All of this can become quite overwhelming.

Many of the apparent roadblocks you'll face as you restore your relationship represent opportunities God places in your path to teach you, correct you, and reveal His vision for your marriage. Some of your roadblocks may occur as a result of the consequences of sins or problems from the past. Still, others are part of a greater spiritual battle. The Enemy wants you to look for a way out of your relationship. He hates a strong marriage. The only way to know what you should do about a roadblock in your relationship is to expose the true nature of it, find out who erected it, and understand the reason(s) it was put there in the first place.

The Road of Restoration

Reread the subtitle above. Note that it says, "The Road *of* Restoration," and not, "The Road *to* Restoration." There's a big difference between the two.

What we are trying to convey here is that the ongoing nature of restoration is a lifestyle and a choice, not simply a destiny or a place at which your marriage will one day arrive. As with any journey, there will be obstacles. Some of these obstacles will be natural and some will be supernatural. You must learn to discern between the two. So did we.

Due to the nature of our divorce and the eleven-year gap that elapsed before we reconciled, we faced some overwhelming obstacles and needed help. As is often the case with couples who reunite, it seemed as if there was roadblock after roadblock in almost every area of our new life together. In desperation, several nights after our initial disagreement, we sat down at the dining room table to make a list of all our roadblocks. Our list included financial burdens, communication problems, family matters, and more. As far as I (Clint) was concerned, these were huge obstacles in our relationship. In hindsight, I now realize that although we thought we'd compiled a pretty complete list that night, it couldn't include the things only God could see coming down the road. It's probably a good thing we didn't know what was about to hit us.

During the first few months of our remarriage, it seemed that every time we turned a corner and made a little headway, we faced yet another challenge. For example, in order to make it to California in time for our wedding, I had driven over 3,000 miles in three days. As a result, I was exhausted. Once I arrived in California, I had to unload my things at Penny's house then go meet the couple who was going to take me in during the days before our wedding. Most of my belongings remained in boxes for weeks and I felt disorganized because I didn't have time to unpack before starting my new job. While I was grateful for a teaching position in the district where Penny was employed, I was still considered a new teacher. Therefore, the district required me to attend special training that started just two days after our wedding. There was no time to be alone with Penny or get away for a honeymoon.

Penny's assignment as an elementary school principal demanded all of her energy and she was used to giving it the time it required. Now, she had a husband to consider. Although she wouldn't admit it, she was struggling to find a balance. In addition to these circumstances, rumors surfaced in our district as to the "real reasons" behind our divorce. The stress began building inside of both of us.

Finances were another huge concern. Penny and I had been apart for such a long time that we didn't realize how awkward it would feel to merge our savings, retirement accounts, and other investments, as well as take on each other's debts. To complicate matters even further, I still had some major burdens from investments that had gone sour while I was living in Florida. In addition, it took six months for my house there to finally sell, so we had two mortgage payments. The resulting stress became so intense for me that, after stuffing it all down inside for several months, I passed out on the locker room floor and school officials had to call for an ambulance. By the time they rushed me to the hospital, massive welts covered my body like continents on a world map. After running some tests, the doctors were able to determine that I'd experienced a rare form of anaphylactic shock. Stress had taken its toll.

Would Our History Repeat Itself?

I (Penny) wanted so much for our marriage to make it this time. After all, I was the one who walked out on Clint so many years earlier. For the first few weeks, I was still in a state of shock about our remarriage. Each morning, I woke up and reached my hand across the bed to make sure Clint was really there. While I was grateful for all that had happened, I also began to experience the self-imposed pressure of wanting to be a better wife this time around. However, I wasn't really sure what a *better wife* was supposed to look like.

In addition to these feelings and my concern over what happened to Clint in the locker room, there were relationships within both of our families that still needed to be healed. Not only had I walked out on Clint all those years ago, but I'd turned my back on his family as well. Our reconciliation called for some awkward face-to-face conversations. I felt so uncomfortable at our first holiday get-together knowing that everyone in Clint's extended family knew the unpleasant details of our divorce. They were very gracious, but I couldn't help feeling like all eyes were on me.

The night we compiled our list of roadblocks at the dining room table, we took turns giving input and adding obstacles to the list. Nothing was too small to be overlooked or invalidated. We included problems such as; handling our different styles of communication, clearing financial debts, finding a new home church, reconciling relationships in our families, and developing the marital values we were missing the first time around. Even though neither of us remarried during our eleven years apart, we still had to deal with the consequences of relationships we'd been involved in during that time. Those issues were also added to our list.

As stated earlier, we were remarried on August 17, 2002. As you will notice, this list was made less than two weeks after our wedding.

Clint and Penny's Roadblocks   **8-29-02**

- The sale of Clint's home in Florida
- Finding a home to call our own
- Friendships with other couples
- A church home we both agree on
- Connections in California for Clint
- Dealing with past relationships/issues
- Balancing our marriage with work
- Communication styles/differences
- Major financial debt

Once we listed our roadblocks, we surrendered each one to God in prayer. While the odds of making it seemed slim-to-none at best, we somehow sensed God's promise to use these roadblocks for purposes we could not yet see. Regardless of how bleak things appeared, after that night we were filled with renewed faith that God would send help. Rather than being paralyzed by our problems, we committed to focusing on God's promises regarding those things.

As the Holy Spirit began to stir our hearts during our individual time in the Word and prayer, God showed us how to progressively chip away at all the things threatening to obstruct our path. Months passed and we kept track of His answers to our prayers on that same piece of paper.

By the end of our first year back together, we noticed significant progress regarding each roadblock that had threatened to obstruct us. More importantly, we were stunned to see that

God had taken every obstacle and used it to show us how to walk through those challenges united as *one flesh*.

As a testimony of God's faithfulness, the power of prayer, and the importance of strengthening our individual relationships with Him, we saved that piece of paper. To this day we reflect on the ways God responded, especially when we need to remember what He'll do when we're humble, intentional, prayerful, willing, obedient, and united. In our current seminars for couples we pull out that list to show them the hard evidence of what God did when we finally took responsibility for our own actions, gave Him full permission to change our hearts, and allowed Him to shape our marriage. God longs to do the same for you as well.

Nehemiah's Roadblocks

Before his work on Jerusalem's wall ever got started, Nehemiah hit his own fair share of roadblocks. In fact, there was so much debris and rubble, it literally blocked his way (Nehemiah 2:14). The bottom line? The prophet was facing an impossible situation. Remember, not only was the wall around the city in ruins and its gates burned by fire, wandering hearts and wayward faith had characterized the Israelite people for generations. Yet, these were the very troops Nehemiah would have to rally in order to begin rebuilding.

It has been said that repairing the wall and the gates around Jerusalem was one of the most monumental rebuilding projects ever undertaken.[3] Prior to making the necessary repairs, Nehemiah took time to carefully survey the damage that had occurred as a result of repeated attacks. He discreetly rode around Jerusalem (most likely by mule or donkey) to inspect the condition of each section, accurately noting what needed to be done.

I went to Jerusalem, and after staying there three days I set out during the night with a few men. I had not told anyone what my God had put in my heart to do for Jerusalem. There were no mounts with me except the one I was riding on. By night I went out through the Valley Gate toward the Jackal Well and the Dung Gate, examining the walls of Jerusalem, which had been broken down, and its gates, which had been destroyed by fire. Then I moved on toward the Fountain Gate and the King's Pool, but there was not enough room for my mount to get through; so I went up the valley by night, examining the wall. Finally, I turned back and reentered through the Valley Gate.

Nehemiah 2:11–15

Since Jerusalem was most often attacked from the north, some scholars say that Nehemiah only surveyed the southern section of the city because it was assumed the northern portion of the wall was completely destroyed. In addition, we can safely speculate that as Nehemiah surveyed the damage, he made important estimates as to the manpower, tools, and time it would take to complete the entire project. This is your charge as well.

Take an Honest Inventory

Like Nehemiah, one of the first things you'll need to do with your spouse is accurately survey the damage done to your relationship. To accomplish this, you must take an honest inventory to identify the roadblocks you're facing at the present time. But remember, you will not engage in this for the purpose of placing blame. Agree right now that you will not throw things

39

from the past in each other's faces. Nothing will hinder your progress faster than trying to hurt each other with old offenses. In addition, ask God to broaden your perspective on your roadblocks through prayer, worship, and His Word. Most importantly, ask the Holy Spirit to help you take an unbiased look at your own heart as it relates to the matters at hand—past and present.

There are no shortcuts to real restoration. We often remind couples that reconciliation is a process, not a series of prescribed steps. More than following a recipe, reconciliation is about following Jesus Christ. Remember, because God created every relationship to be unique, the specific methods He uses to repair one are not necessarily the methods He uses to repair another. One thing can be said of all relationships, however. Honesty is a prerequisite for complete healing.

Be honest with God, yourself, and your spouse. This is not the time to dance around difficult subjects to save face. Humbly admitting past mistakes stimulates mercy, not condemnation, even though you may fear the opposite is true (Proverbs 28:13). The list of roadblocks we made at the dinner table the night we took inventory didn't even include the down and dirty details of our blatant sins. That list would have taken up more than one sheet of paper! Suffice it to say that there were many other strikes against us.

The restoration of your ruins is a time to get real with God, yourself, and each another. Take a look at the way Nehemiah honestly described the state of Jerusalem's wall after he'd surveyed the damage: *"Then I said to them, 'You see the trouble we are in: Jerusalem lies in ruins, and its gates have been burned with fire'"* (Nehemiah 2:17). Notice that he didn't mince words, shrink back in despair, blame others, or become overwhelmed with what he was facing.

40

Remember, neither the destruction from your past nor the roadblocks you face now are a surprise to God. He knows exactly what it's going to take to help your marriage grow into what He envisioned when He created it. For example, imagine our surprise when just moments before the first time we ever shared our testimony of reconciliation in public, I (Penny) noticed the person I'd had the affair with (at the end of our first marriage) was sitting in the audience. Clint and I were shell-shocked, but God wasn't. Instead of bailing out in fear, however, we whispered some reassuring words to each other, united our hearts, and shared our story.

Past hurts and present-day trials will either divide your relationship or draw you closer to God. If you are both growing closer to Him, then you can't help but grow closer to each other. Every time something like what we described above happened (and there were many such incidents), we had an important choice to make. The same goes for you. Your choices, attitudes, actions, and behaviors regarding your trials and circumstances will either hinder true healing or propel you forward. We'll see many examples of this as we continue our study of Nehemiah.

Based on our marriage experiences and those of many other couples, it is better to honestly acknowledge your roadblocks instead of sweeping them under the rug. We're convinced that a significant portion of the problems in our first marriage occurred because we were never totally honest with each other. In retrospect, we realize that regardless of our strong feelings for each other or our faith, we made a critical mistake by not revealing painful experiences from our past or our true feelings about our current problems. We kept secrets from each other. Eventually, those secrets and the consequences of all our life experiences subtly crawled out from under the carpet and crept in between us.

Remaining reconciled is a decision you make *daily*. It's not something that just happens once, after which you proceed to the next thing on your to-do list. No matter what lies ahead, you can be confident that greater than the task at hand is the great hand of God. In the next chapter, we'll help you discover that true wholeness and healing occur not so much from asking God to restore the shattered state of your relationship, but in willingly asking Him to re-tool the state of your individual hearts. That's where the rebuilding really begins.

> *Come, let us rebuild the wall of Jerusalem, and we will no longer be in disgrace. I also told them about the gracious hand of my God upon me and what the king had said to me. They replied, "Let us start rebuilding." So they began this good work.*
>
> Nehemiah 2:17–18

CHAPTER EXERCISES

Prayer to Overcome Obstacles

Father, reveal the changes You want to make in our own hearts regarding our roadblocks. We willingly admit we've sinned and fallen short in our relationship with You and in our marriage. Begin Your work in us and then show us how to overcome the obstacles in our marriage. Help us discern the true nature of our obstacles and how You want us to navigate them. Thoroughly examine our hearts, minds, and motives regarding the ways we can make a positive change in our relationship with You and with each other. Where we have sinned, give us the courage to ask for forgiveness. Where we have wronged You or one another, grant us the desire to humbly apologize and repair these broken places. In the name of Jesus Christ we pray. Amen.

Take an Inventory

Take some time to pray together and ask God to identify the roadblocks you're currently facing in your marriage. Each spouse should make his/her own inventory list first. Then, compare your lists. Identify the similarities and differences between the two. Combine your separate lists and bring each item to God in prayer on a weekly basis. Choose Scripture verses to help guide you in navigating every obstacle. Pray those verses as promises over your problems. Keep track of the movement you notice as God answers your prayers.

Scripture Reading

Read Nehemiah 2 before answering the questions on the next two pages.

Questions to Consider

1. As you look over the inventory you created together, can you identify how each roadblock was initially erected?

2. What positive purposes might each roadblock serve in your relationship now?

3. What did you learn from making your inventory and comparing it to the one your spouse made? As you compared and combined your lists, what similarities and differences surprised you?

4. Are there any secrets or other experiences from your past that still need to be put out on the table? If so, we suggest you schedule a specific time together to pray and discuss these things. If necessary, consider having a trusted mentor, pastor, or counselor assist you with the process of disclosure.

5. List some of the oppositions Nehemiah faced when he first set out to rebuild the wall of Jerusalem. How did he overcome these difficulties and how does this apply to your marriage?

6. Make sure you continue the process of adding positive and negative life events to your marriage timeline. Do you notice any roadblocks from the past that caused conflict between you?

7. How would you currently characterize your individual relationship with God? In the self-assessment below, check the statement that most applies.

Self-Assessment

— Spending time with God in prayer, Bible reading, worship, and fellowship is a high priority in my life each day.

— At least 3-4 times a week, I spend time reading God's Word and praying.

— I seldom spend time alone with God.

— I do not have a personal relationship with God. (If you marked this box, it's important that you speak with a mature Christian or a pastor regarding the desire you have for a personal relationship with God.)

The first ten years of our relationship were very rough. Eventually, our struggles took their toll and we filed for divorce. In one final attempt to save our marriage, we attended a weekend retreat, even though neither of us wanted to go. We thank God for working through the retreat speakers to bring us the exact message of conviction and hope that we needed to hear. In the hotel lobby where the retreat was held, we knelt down in prayer, asked Jesus into our hearts, and gave Him full command over our lives. We asked for God's forgiveness and for His strength to help us build a marriage that would bring Him honor and glory.

Every day since then, we've thanked God for the crisis and pain we went through because that's what brought us to the place of complete brokenness before our Holy God. All the pride, bitterness, anger—everything we were both carrying around—was the bondage that had kept us from experiencing the life God had planned.

Continued on the next page…

Continued from the previous page…

It was our crisis that made us realize our true need for Jesus. Without Christ at the center of our lives and our marriage, we would only end up in bondage to anger, bitterness, and unforgiveness. In the grip of God's grace and in His perfect timing, we finally came to realize that our struggles were more about what God wanted to teach us about us and about Him, than about getting what *we* wanted out of our marriage.

Surrender your heart, your lives, and your marriage to Jesus Christ. Without Him, you will struggle and get nowhere. Without Him, for every step you take forward, your flesh will pull you two steps back. Don't look for a quick fix. Understand that you will need to make a commitment for the long haul and do the work necessary to rebuild (or in some cases, build for the first time) a marriage foundation that has Christ at the center. Get connected to a good local church, one that offers marriage small groups and/or a marriage ministry. Find a solid mentor couple who won't let you slide back into the status quo. And most importantly, PRAY! Pray and ask God to help you and give you what you'll need to build a marriage that will stand the test of time and leave a legacy for future generations.

Carl and Caren Wolfe
Marriage Ministry Leaders
Cornerstone Fellowship
Livermore, CA

Chapter 3 – Forming a Firm Foundation

Although it was frustrating and downright scary to realize there weren't many resources available to guide us when we first reconciled, it forced us to immerse ourselves in God's Word. With our noses in the pages of the Bible, we soon realized the obvious: God is no stranger to reconciliation. Everything we needed to heal our marriage could be found in His Word.

> *Therefore, if anyone is in Christ, he is a new creation; the old has gone, the new has come! All this is from God, who reconciled us to himself through Christ and gave us the ministry of reconciliation: that God was reconciling the world to himself in Christ, not counting men's sins against them. And he has committed to us the message of reconciliation. We are therefore Christ's ambassadors, as though God were making his appeal through us. We implore you on Christ's behalf: Be reconciled to God.*
>
> 2 Corinthians 5:17–20

Webster's dictionary defines the word *reconciliation* as *bringing together again in love, re-establishing a friendship, or reaching a compromise or agreement about your differences or opposing views.* In this passage from 2 Corinthians, the Bible indicates that God desires reconciliation between Himself and His people.

Reconciliation was perfectly modeled when God sent His Son to forgive us and cleanse us from sin (Romans 5:10–11). God's Word also says that He desires reconciled relationships between all believers and that re-establishing relationships in need of healing overtly burdens His heart (Matthew 5:23–24).

The two most important things we noticed about all these passages on reconciling relationships was that God wants us to focus on maintaining a reconciled relationship with Him *first*, before we concern ourselves with each another, and that reconciliation takes action on the part of all the parties involved. Couples often fall into the trap of pointing fingers at one another's faults, falsely assuming the relationship can only be restored if the *other* person changes. It's important to understand, however, that God's first priority is your heart and the improvement of your marriage will naturally follow. Let us share a bit more of our story with you to better illustrate this point.

God's ways of mending our relationship have consistently stretched far beyond what either of us could have comprehended. We still exchange glances in disbelief over what God has done to reconcile us and restore our marriage. But, it wasn't until we focused on our individual relationships with God that He ever reconnected our paths. For many years after our divorce, we'd both run away from God although neither of us knew this because we hadn't seen nor heard from each other after parting ways.

For me (Penny) it was not until eight years after I left Clint that I finally focused my life on God and stopped resisting Him. I vividly remember the night I stretched out my arms, admitted my sins, and asked God to forgive me. After that, I set my entire life and every priority on deepening my relationship with Him through prayer, reading the Bible, worship, and learning from mature believers. I also committed to reconciling the

49

relationships I'd broken. Of course, I was *never* planning to contact Clint. Just the thought was too overwhelming. However, through God's unconditional love and the kindness of believers He placed in my life during that time, the Holy Spirit urged me to take a leap of faith. My intent in finally writing an apology letter to Clint was to tell the truth about what I'd done all those years ago, ask for his forgiveness, and bring closure to that part of the past. Most importantly, I wanted to be obedient in my relationship with God and what His Word said about relationships.

One chilly night in February of 2002, I located Clint's address over the Internet and was stunned to discover he was living over 3,000 miles away in the state of Florida. I could no longer shrug off what God was urging me to do. That night, I wrote the most honest letter that I could, *never* dreaming it would result in our remarriage just six months later.

We'll continue to share bits and pieces of our story with you to illustrate what you'll hear us saying over and over (and over) again throughout the pages of this book. Whatever intricate and intimate details your marriage crisis may involve, focus on daily reconciling your individual relationships with God first. Then, allow Him to guide you regarding the complete restoration of your marriage. Your individual relationships with God must be the foundation of your marriage. Before you begin the process of asking God to reveal His plan for your marriage, you must first ask Him about His plan for your heart. Whether you're a new believer or you've been a Christian for many years, your heart will always remain God's top priority.

Laying the Groundwork

When we were married the first time, we spent all our time *doing* things for God instead of spending time alone with Him. If something needed to be done at church, Penny and I were the first to respond. We were the "church darlings," if you will, and proud of it. While I was busy teaching Sunday school and helping with various projects around the church, Penny was singing in the choir, leading Vacation Bible School, and serving as the Deacon of Missions. Not only was all of our free time tied up at church, but we were each serving in different areas. As a result, we rarely worshiped together or spent quality time with other Christian couples. This oversight perched us for quite a fall. Simply stated, we'd exchanged our intimate relationships with God (and each other) for dutiful service to our church and the accolades that came with it. Although our actions appeared noble at the time, a wedge of pride lodged between us that would eventually split us apart.

We see the same thing happening with couples today. We love the body of Christ and we know how important the church is to the life of a believer and to God's purposes on earth. However, we are also seeing an epidemic of hurting couples in church pews who are slipping through the cracks or hiding behind obligations and committee responsibilities while their marriages are crumbling.

When couples contact us for help, we always begin by asking them about their own personal relationships with God.

"How's your walk with God?" The majority of people give us a blank look as if to say, "What does *that* have to do with my marriage? I want to talk to you about my spouse."

Many people fail to see the direct correlation between the quality of their relationship with God and the relationship with their spouse. We were blind to the correlation between the two the first time around as well. Unbeknownst to either of us at the time, during our years apart, we individually spent time developing the deep spiritual roots we hadn't put down as young converts through focused time in the Word, prayer, and worship. God made sure we'd both learned a lasting lesson from the mistakes we had made in the past. He showed us the direct relationship between the time we spent with Him and the impact of that intimate relationship on everything else in our lives, especially our marriage.

As we open again to the book of Nehemiah as the guide for restoration, we see that this prophet knew the correlation between intimacy with God and relationships with others as evidenced by the following passage:

When I heard these things, I sat down and wept. For some days I mourned and fasted and prayed before the God of heaven. Then I said: "O LORD, God of heaven, the great and awesome God, who keeps his covenant of love with those who love him and obey his commands, let your ear be attentive and your eyes open to hear the prayer your servant is praying before you day and night for your servants, the people of Israel."

Nehemiah 1:4–6

Nehemiah had a personal relationship with God. He knew God and God's commands. He understood the truth about who God was and what He desired for the complete restoration of His covenant with the Israelites. He also realized the odds were stacked against being able to restore Jerusalem and reform its people.

Like Nehemiah, the odds were stacked against our restoration and, to be quite honest, they're stacked against yours, too. However, God doesn't need favorable odds. He's God. Give Him your whole heart and spend time with Him. Learn as much from His Word about love and relationships as you possibly can. Do these things and your healing will come.

As a result of our past mistakes, we learned how essential it is to be intentionally intimate with God every day. After we remarried, we soon realized that, if anything, our individual time with God should increase, not decrease. Most couples do just the opposite. Instead, we urge you to make a conscious decision each day to nurture your individual relationship with God *first*, and then to nurture your mate. This may sound comical, but we make a point of having very little conversation or interaction with each other in the morning until we've both spent time in the Word and prayer. Things seem to run much better that way.

As stated earlier in our introductory letter to this book, all marital dysfunction can be traced back to the soul's deep desire for love and our misguided attempts to find it. Your God-given ache for love can only be satisfied by Him. The same goes for your spouse. When you allow God to fill your hearts with His love and to meet all your needs each day, you'll have an abundance of love to give away. Additionally, the form that loves takes is pure and holy. As He pours into you, you will pour into others. The opposite is also true. If you don't spend time receiving His love and allowing Him to meet your deepest needs, you cannot love others or meet their needs.

The concept of spending time with God sounds relatively simplistic. But as you know, there are many demands calling for your time and attention such as family, work, school, and church. Although these things are extremely important, they can easily crowd out your time with God. If your individual relationship with Him is not in alignment with the Word, the rest of your relationships and responsibilities will suffer, including your marriage.

Going Deeper with God

There are several ways you can nurture intimacy with God. Because time is a scarce commodity in today's families, it's essential that you learn how to maximize your time with Him. Take a look at the items listed below and place a check mark next to the spiritual disciplines you currently engage in on a regular basis. If you're not meeting with God daily, place a check mark next to the things you would like to implement.

Spiritual Disciplines

— Reading the Bible
— Memorizing Scripture verses
— Intercession
— Journaling
— Worship
— Individual Bible study (more than simply reading it)
— Regularly seeking advice from a mature Christian
— Reading Christian literature
— Fasting
— Spending extended periods of time alone with God

There are a variety of different ways your daily time with God can be organized. Many people refer to this as having a "quiet time." When we first became Christians, neither of us really understood what a quiet time entailed. We also got caught up in a legalistic mindset; viewing God more as a task-master and a distant authority figure rather than the Grand Lover who longed to be with us, no matter what our time together "looked" like. What we eventually discovered is that there are many different ways to develop and nurture a more intimate relationship with Him. Of course, this includes reading the Bible and prayer.

Before we get into the specifics of deepening your relationship with God, the most important point we want to reiterate is that your time with Him must be consistent. So often, the tyranny of the urgent threatens to get in the way of this, but that's all the more reason to make your time with Him a definite and intentional priority. If you are not currently spending consistent time with God, start with what we call the *10/10/10 Plan* to give your relationship a jumpstart. The idea is fairly simple. Each day, spend ten minutes reading the Bible, ten minutes journaling in response to what you read, and ten minutes talking and listening to God through prayer.

Again, it's important to remember there are no rules for the way that you spend time with God, except that you should be regularly engaging in the disciplines His Word emphasizes. However, if you need a more specific model to follow (some people operate better that way) the 10/10/10 Plan is one simple way to start structuring this time. Once you've been consistent for several weeks using this format, consider other options and ideas, as well as increasing your time with Him.

Just as with any relationship, the more your love and intimacy develops and deepens, the more you will desire to spend time with Him. Work up to giving God an appropriate tithe (ten percent) of your time. For example, if you are awake for sixteen hours each day, that would equal spending a little over an hour and a half with God. Keep in mind that this time doesn't always have to occur in one sitting. Most people think about a tithe in terms of giving money, but we encourage you to give God a tithe of your time as well.

In order to encourage the tithing of your time, review the following tools we use to deepen our intimacy with God and to build a foundation for our marriage that will last.

Read the Bible

Let's start with the obvious. It's impossible to discover God's will for your life if you don't read the Bible consistently. The reality is that your marriage doesn't have a chance of making it if you aren't willing to commit time to understanding the ways God intended your marriage to function. Even reading a Psalm or a Proverb each day will make a significant difference in your life and your relationship with your spouse. Again, if you need a more structured approach to reading, there are various Bible reading plans available on the Internet (see page 298 for a list of online resources). Many of these plans are designed so that you will read through the entire Bible in one year. There are also several one-year Bibles you can purchase at your local Christian bookstore or online bookseller if that kind of structure suits you.

Eventually, an honorable goal would be to read the Word in a way that accurately reflects your intimate relationship with God. Remember, it's not important to measure your Bible reading in quantity (how much you read), but in quality (how you read and apply it to your life).

Memorize Scripture

Memorizing Bible verses shouldn't be relegated to something little children do in Sunday school. Now more than ever, you need to have God's promises hidden in the recesses of your heart and ready on the tip of your tongue. Start slowly. Select one or two verses to memorize each week. Ask God for the verses He wants you to memorize. You may find it helpful to select verses that have to do with relationships or more specifically, marriage.

To help you memorize Scripture, write out the verses on index cards and place them in several prominent locations around your workplace and/or home. Laminating these cards will make them more durable. Pray through the words of the verse(s) you're memorizing as you go through the week so that they become a part of your dialogue back to God. For example:

Memory Verse: *"And my God will meet all your needs according to his glorious riches in Christ Jesus"* (Philippians 4:19).

Prayer Dialogue: God, I believe You will meet all my needs and I rely on You to do so today, in every area of my life.

The more you practice doing this, the more comfortable and natural it will become. Praying your memory verse(s) back to God is a powerful way to communicate your trust in Him. Because His Word is alive and active, your prayers will stir the Holy Spirit to respond and you'll become more steadfast and resilient when challenges arise.

Pray Often
Prayer is so essential to maintaining reconciled relationships that we've devoted a whole chapter to it (see Chapter 5). However, we'll briefly state a few basics about prayer here as well. One simple thing we've incorporated into our marriage is that we don't leave the house in the morning until we've spent two or three minutes in prayer together. Mind you, a few minutes don't seem like much, but God has honored this commitment. Praying together each morning has given us a sense of God's complete control and sovereignty over our marriage.

Many people maintain a prayer list or journal to remind them of the people and circumstances about which they're praying and to help them develop a more thorough prayer life. At times, we change up our prayer lives to keep our conversations with God fresh. Sometimes, we use a prayer list and sometimes we toss the list aside and pray as the Holy Spirit leads. However, we both consistently keep a prayer journal as a way of tracing God's hand. At times, keeping a journal or prayer list may seem overwhelming. If you're a person who needs some structure, one option is to arrange your prayer life into a daily format. For example:

My Prayer List

Monday – Pray for your spouse, marriage, and family.
Tuesday – Pray for your friends.
Wednesday – Pray for your pastors and your church.
Thursday – Pray for your co-workers, classmates, etc.
Friday – Pray for the unsaved people in your life.
Saturday – Pray for world leaders, missionaries, and global concerns.
Sunday – Give thanks to God in prayer for all the blessings He's bestowed upon you.

If you use a format such as the one written above, we do suggest that you pray for your marriage every day, not just once a week.

Eventually, your goal should be that prayer becomes as automatic and necessary as breathing. However, it takes time to develop an impulsivity to pray at all times. You learn to pray by praying...and praying…and praying again. We'll speak more specifically about integrating prayer into your marriage as the book progresses.

Keep a Journal

Penny and I have kept journals for years. When we first reconciled, sharing past journal entries was an incredible way to see how God had divinely orchestrated our intersection after of all our years apart. In our work with couples, we've discovered that journaling seems to be used by women more often than men. However, I tell guys about how God changed me from being a person who didn't like to write *anything*, to a man who can't go a day without opening his journal to write. My journal is reserved for the sole purpose of intercession. My mind has less of a tendency to wander during prayer if I write down my prayers. In my journal I pray about my relationship with God, Penny, and concerns related to our friends, family, ministry, and any other things on my heart. I also like to spend time writing down my praises to God in my journal.

Penny uses her journal to express her feelings and thoughts to God. In it, she responds to His Word, our marriage, family, friends, and other events that transpire in her life. As of this writing, she's filled over forty journals that span a period of approximately thirty years.

A journal should be used in a way that suits you best. In order to teach couples the value and discipline of responding to God's Word and keeping track of their daily relationships with Him, we've developed a simple model as a starting point.

- **Record** Scripture verse(s) from your Bible reading time.
- **Relate** that/those verse(s) to your own life.
- **Respond** to God by writing a prayer.
- **Rejoice** and give thanks to God for something.

Here is one example of what this model might look like in your daily journal:

My Journal

Record: *"I consider that our present sufferings are not worth comparing with the glory that will be revealed in us"* (Romans 8:18).

Relate: God, when I get busy during the day and trials come, I forget that what I'm dealing with is nothing compared to what I have to look forward to when I spend eternity in Heaven with You.

Respond: Dear God, please remind me that I have an eternal hope to look forward to each day. When the challenges come, may I remember that my struggles have a divine purpose. In Jesus' name I pray. Amen.

Rejoice: I'm grateful for Your Word. You are always faithful to hear my prayers and keep Your promises. Thank You for being patient with me.

If you want your journal time to be less structured and more open-ended, consider using some of these journal prompts.

Dear God,

- I just wanted to take a moment to say…
- I am concerned about what I should do regarding…
- I want to thank You for…
- What do You think about…
- Do You think I should…
- I'm sorry for…
- I was wondering if…
- One of the things I appreciate about Your love is…
- If I could see You face-to-face right now, I would…
- I think I've been reluctant to…
- I want to commit to You that I will…

Worship God Daily

Many people think worship is something that only takes place at church or in a large group setting. But you can worship God in many ways, all by yourself. Worshiping God means you're putting Him in His rightful place—lifted up and magnified. Worship causes an immediate shift in your perspective and can take many forms because worship is anything that gives God glory; like singing, reading Psalms aloud, or listening to music that edifies Him. Like prayer, worship can be done anytime and anywhere because it is an attitude of your heart, reflected in everything you do.

I (Penny) love to have private worship time; to be shut away from others and totally alone so that I can express my love and gratitude to God. But, when duty calls and I must minister, run errands, complete chores around the house, etc., I ask God to help me worship Him *through* those activities. I've finally discovered that even the most mundane tasks can be transformed into a form of worship. When worshiping God is the attitude and intent of your heart, you can worship Him no matter where you are or what you're doing. Like developing your prayer life, developing creative ways to worship God takes time and practice.

Engage in Individual Bible Study

Studying the Bible is different than simply reading it. Studying the Bible means digging deeper into its meaning, historical context, and application. There are many resources available today to help you study the Bible at a deeper level. If you've never participated in a small group Bible study, start there. Ask your pastor or other people for suggestions. Most churches have several Bible studies and small groups that might be of interest to you. From there, branch out into studying specific books of the Bible or passages of Scripture in more depth on your own.

Purchasing a study Bible dramatically changed my relationship with God. The cross-references and footnotes enabled me to decipher the deeper meanings in the Bible. Reading and studying several translations of the Bible has also been imperative to knowing and understanding His will. Simply looking up a passage and reading it in three or four different translations increases my knowledge and understanding of who God is and how I can more effectively apply His Word to my life.

Read Christian Literature

There are literally thousands of great Christian books on the market today. There are also many daily devotionals that are easy to follow. (Visit your local Christian bookstore or an online bookseller for additional suggestions and see page 299 for a recommended list of devotionals). Consider selecting a book to read with your spouse. We do this often and enjoy discussing what we're reading and how it applies to our lives. We take turns selecting a book to read and purchase two copies. Then, we read a chapter or two each week and discuss what we're reading. (For more information on reading books together, see Chapter 11.)

Utilize the Discipline of Fasting

Fasting means to abstain from something (usually food) for spiritual purposes. The Bible contains many examples of people who engaged in the discipline of fasting such as Moses, David, Elijah, Esther, and Daniel, just to name a few. Take some time to read Isaiah 58. In that chapter, you will discover a direct correlation between fasting and restoration as well as a clear explanation of the kind of fasting that truly honors God.

Even Jesus fasted during his time on earth (Matthew 4:2). Fasting, combined with prayer, is a powerful way to nurture intimacy in your relationship with God, but it requires proper preparation and pure motives. Unfortunately, of all the spiritual disciplines, fasting is the least popular simply because it isn't fully understood. People think about what they'll have to do without rather than about what God will do through fasting and prayer.

Researching all the biblical accounts of fasting is a good way to get started with investigating this discipline. There are also many outstanding Christian books that explain what fasting is and what it's not. We recommend that you do some reading prior to fasting so you'll have a greater understanding of how God intended it to be practiced.

Some people can't fast due to a medical condition. You should consult your doctor prior to fasting if health issues are a concern. If you are unable to fast from food, ask God to show you other things from which you can abstain. For example, you can agree with your spouse to fast from the use of negative comments, judgmental overtones, or critical thoughts. Agreeing to engage in a fast of this sort is a very powerful way to get in alignment with God's Word. Couples who fast and pray together unlock the doors to a whole new dimension in their spiritual lives.

Get Alone with God

Some of our most significant spiritual experiences occur when we set aside long blocks of time or even an entire day to spend with God in prayer, Bible study, journaling, reading, and worshiping. If you've never taken a day off for just you and God, this may take some practice. Many people ask, "What would I do with God all day?" Spending extended time with God is not just about what you do with God, but, more importantly, what God will do with you.

Start praying about this idea and let Him lead you. Turn off your cell phone and leave your e-mail for another day. If you aren't sure about how to spend time alone with Him, ask other Christians what they do. Start with a few hours and work your way up to a full day or even a weekend. There are many Christian conference centers that offer structured retreats in which participants are given time and resources to get away with God. (In Chapter 11, we'll discuss effective ways to get away with God as a couple.)

In Hot Pursuit

Chances are that when you met and fell in love with your spouse, a pursuit ensued. You courted and spent time getting to know one another's history, dislikes, desires, and dreams. You invested in becoming a part of each other's lives because you were in love. Our challenge to you is to pursue God just like that. Court Him. Date Him. Spend time getting to know His Word, His history with man, His miracles and wonders, and His dislikes and desires.

Again, we can't stress how important it is to focus on God first and foremost at all times. When conflicts arise, the tendency is to focus on your spouse or on the crisis itself. However, God wants you to seek Him first and let Him be in charge of everything else (Matthew 6:33). As you spend time with God and become an active and willing participant in the processes He is using to make you holy, positive changes in your heart will occur, regardless of your circumstances.

If you're not spending time in the Word and prayer each day, it will be impossible to see significant changes in your marriage. Now, more than ever, you need to buckle down and spend some extra quality time with Him. One suggestion is to take whatever time you are spending with God right now and, in a step of faith, double it for the next forty days. Give God a double portion of your time and expect Him to honor your efforts out of His grace and love for you. In the next chapter, we'll look at some tangible ways to keep your marriage properly aligned to the promises and precepts in His Word so that even when trials come, you'll remain steadfast on the road of reconciliation.

CHAPTER EXERCISES

Prayer to Form a Firm Foundation
Father, we want to deepen our knowledge of You. We realize part of the reason we may be going through trials in our relationship is that You want to get our attention and teach us something about who You are. We don't quite know where to begin pursuing You so we're asking You to help us extend and deepen the time we are spending with You each day. Show us how to lay a firm foundation in our marriage. Teach us how to spend quality time with You in a way that pleases You and keeps us in the center of Your will. Help us incorporate some new ideas into our relationships with You and teach us how to make this practice more of a priority.

Making a Connection
Pursuing God's presence is something you'll do for the rest of your life. It's important to ask other Christians what they do to nurture spiritual intimacy. Between now and next week, ask one or two people what they do to deepen their relationship with Him. Share your discoveries with your spouse.

Scripture Reading
Read Nehemiah 3 and 4 before answering the questions on the next page.

Questions to Consider

1. Were there any ideas in this chapter that sparked your interest or curiosity? Share those with your spouse.

2. What are some of the things from this chapter you'll consider using in your relationship with God this week? Share your plans with a trusted friend and ask him/her to pray for your quiet time during the coming week.

3. What progress is made regarding the rebuilding of Jerusalem's wall and what problems does Nehemiah encounter?

4. Take out your marriage timeline and add any spiritual life events to it. Positive spiritual events may include things such as the salvation of a family member, baptisms, or finding a new home church. Negative spiritual life events might include the loss of a loved one, a crisis of faith, or a conflict that upset you and/or other members of your church.

Paul and Linda were divorced one month after their eighteenth anniversary.

"I never thought we should have divorced," shared Paul. Soon after we went our separate ways, I was filled with the hope that, one day, Linda and I would remarry. We were both raised in Christian homes. What we'd done was against God's will and deep down, we both knew it. Our divorce lasted sixteen months. Then, it was as if God grabbed our attention and let us *both* know that we had to take responsibility for what we had done."

Linda continued. "God showed us how we got into trouble because we hadn't put Christ at the center of our marriage. When I asked God to restore our marriage, He gave me more of a husband and marriage than I could have ever imagined. I couldn't have asked for the forgiveness, regaining of trust, healing, and restoration He provided."

"I knew that I was a changed man," said Paul, "and that I'd be a better husband because of what we went through. Our reconciliation was definitely a God thing. It was the Bible that brought us back to our roots. Together, we vowed to keep Christ in the center of our lives and marriage the second time around. Our hunger for Christ began to increase and we desperately wanted a marriage that would be grounded in the Word."

"There are several ways Paul and I have kept our marriage fixed on God's Word during the eleven years we've now been remarried. After breakfast each morning, we lay out all our thanksgivings and petitions, and then put on the whole armor of God.

Continued on the next page…

Throughout the day as we sit down to work on projects or have major decisions to make, we pray beforehand, which keeps the standards in His Word at the center of our lives and work. Before retiring at night, we have a devotional time which also keeps God at the forefront of our relationship. This encourages us to discuss the things we normally wouldn't have time to talk about during the day.

"The three main biblical standards that Linda and I have in our marriage consist of keeping pure in heart, spending time in the Word, and praying together. There are also several verses at the core of who we are as husband and wife. Ephesians 5:25 says, 'Husbands, love your wives, just as Christ loved the church and gave himself up for her.' We see this as the ultimate sacrificial love that says, 'I'll die for you.' This standard brings real meaning to the unconditional love we share."

"Another meaningful verse is Genesis 2:24. 'For this reason a man will leave his father and mother and be united to his wife, and they will become one flesh.' This verse represents a sharing-of-the-heart type of love that says, 'I will never leave you and we will walk life together as one.' These standards weren't part of us in our first marriage, but they're the foundation of our reconciliation. God is amazing and He has done incredible things in our lives for which we're very thankful."

'Now to Him who is able to do immeasurable more than all we ask or imagine, according to His power that is at work within us' (Ephesians 3:20).

Paul and Linda Geyer
AMFM Marriage Ambassadors
Phoenix, AZ

Chapter 4 – Synchronizing Your Standards

Have you ever driven a vehicle that wasn't properly aligned? If so, it probably veered off the highway to one side or the other and it took a firm grip on the wheel to drive safely, right? Any experienced driver will testify that in order for a car to travel straight down the road, the front-end must be properly aligned and the tires balanced. The same can be said for your marriage. If your marriage isn't in proper alignment with the standards found in God's Word, all it takes are a few bumps in the road for the relationship to veer off course. In contrast, husbands and wives who come together and make a deliberate, daily attempt to align their relationship with God's standards will discover the important keys to developing a more resilient relationship.

When Clint and I were married in 1989, we were both Christians. We attended church regularly and served God in many different ways. As far as we were concerned, we thought that was enough to make for a strong marriage. But, we were wrong. When challenges began to arise between us, we didn't know what to do because we were immature in our faith and hadn't spent much time rooting our marriage in God's Word.

To complicate matters, we were too proud and embarrassed to tell anyone that our marriage was on shaky ground. When our pastor finally found out, I already had one foot out the door. It wasn't until we were remarried that we came to understand how our marriage must be in complete alignment with the principles in the Bible.

What's Your Standard?

For the purposes of this book, let's define the word, *standard,* as: *the criterion on which your marriage is based.* Think of standards as the agreed-upon focal points of your relationship. In Chapter 11, we'll discuss the ways your marriage standards become the bar by which progress in your relationship is measured. For now, let's just establish what the standards are for a Christ-based marriage and the ways in which these should play out in your everyday lives.

Subconsciously, everyone brings their own standards into a marriage. These standards are based on several things such as: childhood/upbringing, marriage role models, past experiences, values, attitudes, culture, and beliefs. Chances are that neither you nor your spouse were consciously aware of the standards you brought into your marriage or from where they originated. For example, where did you derive your concepts about the division of roles and responsibilities in your household? Or, what about the way conflict should be handled, your spending/saving habits, or your ideas about parenting? Consider the characteristics of the marriages surrounding you when you were growing up. How did those role models impact your views on marriage?

Reflect for a few moments on the standards you possessed before becoming husband and wife. What did you think your roles and responsibilities should look like? What did you assume your spouse's role would be? Did you imagine having conflict in your relationship? Did you consider the ways in which you would work together to resolve problems? Did you have expectations for your relationship based on your childhood upbringing? How do your answers to these questions compare with those of your spouse?

Based on our experiences and those of the couples we've worked with over the years, a high percentage of the conflicts that divide a marriage come from the fact that the standards each spouse brought into the relationship are different. As a result, the manifestation (the everyday acting out) of these differences creates conflict. Although this may sound grossly over-simplified, we know it to be true. Let us give you a concrete example from our first marriage.

I (Penny) grew-up in a large Italian family with six children. When there was a conflict or crisis, everyone (including my extended family members) knew about it and each person had an opinion to contribute. Arguments were loud occasions, to say the least. Body language was demonstrative, emotions were dramatic, and explanations were exaggerated. The issue at hand was discussed with great gusto until it was resolved. Coming to a resolution of any sort was a long and involved process. So naturally, my approach to dealing with conflict closely mirrored the model from my childhood.

Clint, on the other hand, was raised with a drastically different model for conflict resolution. His only sibling was his younger sister and his parents were very reserved. His family is of German descent. If there was a problem, it was settled quickly and quietly and more often than not, behind closed doors. What little discussion a problem may have required tended to be void of high emotion. With these two drastically different families of origin, you can probably imagine what happened the first time Clint and I had a disagreement.

In addition to these kinds of scenarios, many people never realize that they are likely to experience a *cultural clash* when they marry. A large percentage of the standards or norms you bring into marriage come from your cultural background and ethnicity. These differences may be more overt, such as skin color or language, or they may be more subtle, such as communication styles or family traditions. Whatever the case, cultural differences can be the source of intense conflict and will quickly zap your marriage of unity if those differences are not brought into submission under God.

Veering Off Course

During our first marriage, I remember feeling very confused as to why Clint was so reluctant to discuss a particular problem we were having. The more I persisted in wanting to talk through our differences, the more Clint shut-down. As a result, my emotions grew steamy which only served to make matters worse. The night of our first major argument, we went to bed without having resolved the conflict and I cried myself to sleep feeling disillusioned and misunderstood. When I woke up the next morning, it seemed like there were miles between us, instead of just inches. Figuring I'd given Clint enough time to think, I brought the matter up again, before the first cup of coffee was poured.

"So, what are we going to do about this?" I asked, hoping to come to some kind of compromise. Clint said nothing. Instead, he walked into the kitchen and made something to eat. As I had done the night before, I started filling up every molecule of air space with my opinions and emotions, determined to find the resolution that seemed to elude us. It never came. Conflicts after that only widened the existing gap between us. During our brief first marriage, every conflict we had seemed to get snagged in the same cycle.

Looking back, neither of us can remember the exact sources of our discontent. What we remember is the drastically different manner by which we approached resolving conflict and how it stemmed from our upbringing. Herein is the problem most couples face. The manner of dealing with conflict for one spouse (his/her *standards* for conflict resolution) is not the same as that of the other.

Shortly after we were remarried, we realized that *synchronizing* our standards for conflict resolution to those found in God's Word would create a much more well-rounded, resilient, and harmonious relationship; one that honored God, even in the midst of conflict.

Nehemiah spoke of something similar when he set out to reform the Israelites and rebuild their community.

> *Remember the instruction you gave your servant Moses, saying, "If you are unfaithful, I will scatter you among the nations, but if you return to me and obey my commands, then even if your exiled people are at the farthest horizon, I will gather them from there and bring them to the place I have chosen as a dwelling for my Name."*
>
> Nehemiah 1:8–9

Being dispersed and exiled was a consequence of not having their lives and relationships in alignment with the laws and commands God set down for them through Moses. Their disobedience resulted in broken relationships. Of utmost importance was their fractured covenant with God. And, not living in alignment with His standards directly impacted their relationships with each other. In Nehemiah 5, we see another example of what happens when our interactions with God and one another are not in alignment with His standards.

Now the men and their wives raised a great outcry against their Jewish brothers. Some were saying, "We and our sons and daughters are numerous; in order for us to eat and stay alive, we must get grain." Others were saying, "We are mortgaging our fields, our vineyards and our homes to get grain during the famine." Still others were saying, "We have had to borrow money to pay the king's tax on our fields and vineyards. Although we are of the same flesh and blood as our countrymen and though our sons are as good as theirs, yet we have to subject our sons and daughters to slavery. Some of our daughters have already been enslaved, but we are powerless, because our fields and our vineyards belong to others."

Nehemiah 5:1–5

Nehemiah had his hands full. Food was scarce and taxes were high. The Jews were so engaged in rebuilding the city that they were not completing the daily tasks necessary to maintain their own households. As a result, many people were forced to mortgage property to those who were in the business of lending. For a while, borrowing from their brethren didn't seem to be problematic. However, once the initial euphoria of the task at hand wore off, conflict arose that threatened to put a screeching halt to the rebuilding. By the time Nehemiah became aware of this problem, the disagreement had gotten completely out of hand.

It's important to notice from the passage that the opposition wasn't coming at Nehemiah from an outside source (as indicated in other passages) but from within the community of people he was attempting to help. Imagine what it must have been like to be right in the middle of this monumental project, only to have a major outbreak of frustration, fear, and dissention amongst your

75

co-laborers! Make no mistake: Satan was determined to do whatever he could to interrupt the rebuilding process by splintering their relationships. The same holds true for our marriages today. The Enemy longs for our interactions and relationships to get out of alignment with God's Word and His ways. It doesn't take much to cause a great divide.

We can learn a valuable lesson from the way Nehemiah went about getting God's people back into alignment with His laws. Look at his response to the conflict:

> *When I heard their outcry and these charges, I was very angry. I pondered them in my mind and then accused the nobles and officials. I told them, "You are exacting usury from your own countrymen!" So I called together a large meeting to deal with them and said: "As far as possible, we have bought back our Jewish brothers who were sold to the Gentiles. Now you are selling your brothers, only for them to be sold back to us!" They kept quiet, because they could find nothing to say. So I continued, "What you are doing is not right. Shouldn't you walk in the fear of our God to avoid the reproach of our Gentile enemies? I and my brothers and my men are also lending the people money and grain. But let the exacting of usury stop! Give back to them immediately their fields, vineyards, olive groves and houses, and also the usury you are charging them—the hundredth part of the money, grain, new wine and oil."*
>
> Nehemiah 5:6–11

Nehemiah knew God required something contrary to the ways His people were treating each another and he wasn't afraid to call them on it. He brought the Jews into account by reminding them of God's expectations and standards for relationships. Look at the way the people responded to Nehemiah's realignment of their behavior: *"We will give it back," they said. "And we will not demand anything more from them. We will do as you say"* (Nehemiah 5:12).

Coming into Alignment

In order for God to restore your marriage, it's imperative that you take an honest look at the standards you subconsciously brought into your marriage and come to an agreement to do the work necessary to base your marriage on God's standards; the promises and principles found in His Word.

For starters, you can begin this process by learning what God's standards are and then, making a conscious effort to integrate them into your marriage. As discussed in the last chapter, this happens naturally when you spend consistent time in God's Word. God makes the transformation and blending of our differences possible through the gift of His Holy Spirit working in cooperation with His Word. Once those changes begin to occur, God's standards need to be applied to your relationships and circumstances through obedience and faith.

Look at the example on the following page which contains two of the standards we've agreed upon as part of the *criterion* for our new marriage. Notice that each standard is matched with a verse or passage of Scripture. That way, we're certain the standards in our marriage are aligned with those in the Bible.

Standard 1: We will forgive one another's past mistakes and present-day faults. Nothing in the past will be thrown in each other's faces. *"Therefore, as God's chosen people, holy and dearly loved, clothe yourselves with compassion, kindness, humility, gentleness and patience. Bear with each other and forgive whatever grievances you may have against one another. Forgive as the Lord forgave you"* (Colossians 3:12–13).

Standard 2: We commit to never speak rudely, harshly, or disrespectfully to each another, in public or private. *"Do not let any unwholesome talk come out of your mouths, but only what is helpful for building others up according to their needs, that it may benefit those who listen"* (Ephesians 4:29).

Developing our marriage standards didn't happen overnight, but over a period of several months. One of the ways we started developing standards for our marriage was to simply begin praying about it. When we asked God to reveal the places in our marriage that were out of alignment with His Word, it didn't take long for a list to begin forming. We also looked honestly at the areas of our greatest disagreements and discrepancies. For example, given the differences in the ways our families of origin dealt with conflict, we knew we needed a standard to help us handle our disagreements appropriately. Not my way. Not Clint's way. But, *God's* way.

During our time in the Word, we took note of the verses that exemplified the ways we wanted to interact with each other. Then, we developed a standard to reflect what we were reading. As an added bonus, the process we went through to ensure that our marriage was based on God's standards meant that we were spending time in the Word together. We were also enjoying some deep conversations about our relationship and God's vision for our marriage.

We also talked with several Christian couples we respected because they seemed to have stable and godly marriages. We observed their interactions and discussed the aspects of these relationships that we desired for our own. Taking note of the couples who interacted in a manner we didn't like and discussing the ways we didn't want our marriage to reflect that sort of negative behavior was also important.

We've created a collection of sample marriage standards that you may find useful. We share these with you in order to give you a better idea of how God's Word can play out in your marriage every day.

Sample Marriage Standards

- We will love one another and joyfully fulfill our marriage vows of lifetime fidelity.
- We will be as polite and courteous to one another as we are to our friends and colleagues.
- We will abstain from the use of any form of pornography or the viewing of degrading movies, television programs, websites, or other inappropriate media.
- We will thank God for our meals before we partake of them.
- We will faithfully and regularly attend worship services and serve together.

Sample Marriage Standards (continued)

- We will work out our conflicts, challenges, and problems in truth and honesty, without unhealthy interference or excess drama from relatives or friends.
- We will give to others from a generous heart; tithing at least ten percent of our income to God, and working out a shared partnership in regard to all purchases, expenses, and other financial matters.
- We will humbly dedicate our lives, family, home, and material possessions to Christ and practice His teachings by being loyal, loving, and generous in all circumstances.
- We will maintain and cultivate a healthy sense of humor and engage in common activities together.

Some of the couples we've met over the years have actually written down their standards, framed them, and hung them up in their homes. Others have expanded their standards to include some for parenting and extended family relationships. You may choose to call your children together so everyone can have input as to how the family should function based on God's Word.

Getting Down to the Nitty Gritty

Because our marriage history contained some major offenses, we found it necessary to develop some standards that specifically spoke to those issues. This may be true for you as well. For example, it was important for us to have a standard that reflected forgiveness and an agreement never to dredge up the past in order to hurt each other. Of course, it was easy to find some Bible verses that matched with standards of forgiveness and mercy.

Sometimes, you may wish to start with a Bible verse and write a standard based on it. Or, you can start with an idea and find the appropriate Scripture to reflect what you are trying to say about your marriage. Continue the process of developing your marriage standards and finding the corresponding Scripture verses until you have a comprehensive list of what matters most to God regarding your relationship. We also suggest that you look at the places of past pain (for example; infidelity, rage, dishonesty) and specifically compose standards for those issues. This is an important key to not repeating past mistakes.

Nehemiah took a similar course with the Israelites, once he brought them back into alignment with God's laws and convinced them to stop taking advantage of one another and repeating the inappropriate behavior from their past.

Then I summoned the priests and made the nobles and officials take an oath to do what they had promised. I also shook out the folds of my robe and said, "In this way may God shake out of his house and possessions every man who does not keep this promise. So may such a man be shaken out and emptied!" At this the whole assembly said, "Amen," and praised the LORD. And the people did as they had promised.
Nehemiah 5:12–13

When Nehemiah shook out the folds of his robe, he was making a strong symbolic statement as to what would happen if the people returned to their old patterns of behavior, such as idol worship and a blatant disregard for God's commands. Part of the challenge of making certain your marriage remains focused on biblically-based standards is to find creative ways to regularly integrate them into your marriage and family. It's not enough to write them down and never revisit them again. After you have developed your marriage standards, it will be important to continue reviewing them so they remain the foundation of your marriage and family. In order to do this, you may find it helpful to engage in the following activities on a regular basis:

Integrating Standards into Your Marriage

- Pray over your standards weekly. Allow God to examine your heart for areas that may be out of alignment with His Word and to reveal the ways your behavior needs to change.
- Use these standards to help you make wise decisions and to stay focused on what matters most.
- Meditate on and memorize the verses you selected for your standards.
- Ask a trusted Christian couple to hold you accountable to fulfilling your marriage standards. Give them a copy of your standards as well as your permission to ask about the ways your marriage is growing, changing, or struggling.

Once you've completed the process of developing your marriage standards, commit them to God and promise each another to hold tightly to what you've agreed upon for the remainder of your lives together. Consider a prayer of dedication as you agree to adhere to these commitments. From time to time, you will find it necessary to amend your marriage standards as your relationship deepens and as you encounter trials and circumstances you haven't dealt with before.

Basing our marriage on God's standards has undeniably transformed our relationship the second time around. It took work, discussion, practice, failure, and a lot of prayer. However, eventually we noticed that our greatest concerns were no longer about getting our own way, but about making certain we both respected and honored God's ways. As time has passed and we've learned how to cover our marriage standards with times of regular prayer, God has absolutely blown the lid off of our relationship. Integrating prayer into every aspect of our marriage has allowed for the complete restoration and redemption from the pain of our past and has launched our marriage into brand new territory. Effectively, creatively, and faithfully integrating prayer into your marriage will be the subject of the next chapter.

CHAPTER EXERCISES

Prayer to Synchronize Your Standards

God, we understand that we each brought our own standards into our marriage and some of them weren't in alignment with Your Word. We want to make a change. Our desire is to have a marriage based on the principles and promises in the Bible. Reveal the areas of our relationship on which You want us to focus. Lead us to the Scripture verses You want us to use as our foundation. May the power of Your Holy Spirit align our hearts and minds with Yours so that we come to agreements that will honor You. We believe our marriage will be restored when we steadfastly base all of our interactions on the standards found in Your Word. In Jesus' name we pray. Amen.

Come Together

Take some time to pray together, search God's Word, and write at least eight-to-ten standards for your marriage. Don't try to accomplish this in one sitting. You may wish to use the samples of standards from this chapter and combine them with some of your own. Each standard should be accompanied by a corresponding Bible verse or passage. After you have written your marriage standards, pray over them, giving God the opportunity to change or refine them further, if necessary. When you're ready, type the final standards and corresponding Bible verses onto a piece of paper, frame them, and place them prominently in your home. You may wish to share in a time of commitment and communion together as well. This is a memorable spiritual event for families to engage in and can become a treasured part of your spiritual legacy.

Scripture Reading

Review Nehemiah Chapters 1-6 and take specific note of the ways the prophet used prayer to make progress on the restoration of the wall around Jerusalem and the reformation of the Jewish community.

Questions to Consider

1. What are some of the standards you brought into your marriage regarding the roles and responsibilities of husbands and wives? Your standards regarding spending habits? Handling conflict? Cultural traditions? From where/whom did these originate?

2. What or who is the current focus of your marriage? Explain your answer. (Note: The answer will likely tell you upon what or whom your marriage is currently based.)

3. What have you noticed thus far regarding Nehemiah's determination and attitude toward the opposition he faced during the rebuilding project?

4. How might Nehemiah's approach to his problems apply to the restoration of your marriage?

5. As you continue adding positive and negative life events to the marriage timeline you started in Chapter 1, can you identify the ways biblical standards might have stabilized your relationship during tough times and conflicts? Can you identify how the standards you possessed prior to marrying played into the struggles with your spouse?

After we were saved and got remarried, there was still a lack of understanding about how important prayer was to our restoration. Due to our two failed marriages to each other, we certainly had our work cut out for us. There was so much to learn and by the grace of God, we learned it.

We started using prayer to restore our marriage by remembering to regularly thank God for saving us and bringing us back together. Eventually, we also learned how to use prayer to resolve our disagreements. Even now when difficulties arise in our relationship, we take a "strife break," find a verse or passage from the Bible that applies to our situation, and pray together about the problem.

During our daily devotions, we join hands and pray. Holding hands gives us both a physical and a spiritual connection. Sometimes, we also pray a blessing over each other before the day begins. Throughout the week, there are many times when we intercede for each other as new situations arise.

It is our passion to teach others the skills we wish we would have learned a long time ago. As we travel and minister to couples in need, we encourage them to use Scripture that applies to their situation and to take time out from the conflict to pray together. Most of all we remind them that all things are possible through Christ.

Pastor Joe and Gerri Begay
Grace Fellowship Community Church
Chinle, AZ

Chapter 5 – Using Prayer as a Power Tool

But when Sanballat, Tobiah, the Arabs, the Ammonites and the men of Ashdod heard that the repairs to Jerusalem's walls had gone ahead and that the gaps were being closed, they were very angry. They all plotted together to come and fight against Jerusalem and stir up trouble against it. But we prayed to our God.

Nehemiah 4:7–9

Nehemiah knew exactly how to deal with the circumstances threatening to interrupt the rebuilding of Jerusalem's walls. When challenges arose, he fought off his foes and silenced their accusations by praying and continuing the work God called him to complete. Throughout the book of Nehemiah, we see evidence that of all the tools in his tool belt, prayer was, by far, this prophet's most powerful and valuable resource.

They were all trying to frighten us, thinking, "Their hands will get too weak for the work, and it will not be completed." But I prayed, "Now strengthen my hands."

Nehemiah 6:9

Like our prayerful prophet, intercession must be an essential power tool that is regularly used to keep our marriages in consistent alignment with God's standards. Ideally, your prayer life will be most effective and life-changing when it is a part of *everything* you do as husband and wife. Like breathing, prayer must become something you engage in constantly; almost subconsciously and without hesitation or reservation.

If you want to take your prayer life as husband and wife to the next level, we have some suggestions for you in this chapter. But, beware! These tools are not for the faint of heart. When you join together in prayer, you give God permission to radically restore and transform your marriage. There are few things that move the heart of God more than husbands and wives who pray together.

Facing Each Day with Prayer

As is often the case, it took a major crisis for Penny and me to finally realize the true power of praying together. Several months after we remarried, a frightening incident took place at the middle school where I was teaching. In the midst of dealing with an ongoing investigation and a lot of red tape, we decided to pray together before I left for school one morning. After Penny and I finished praying, we parted ways. As the miles passed on my commute, I felt an overwhelming sense of God's peace permeating my heart and mind. This peace remained inside me throughout the entire day and the difficult circumstances I was facing at school were getting ironed out much more quickly than anticipated.

When I got home that evening, I told Penny about the peace I experienced because of our prayer time together and that the problem at school was quickly getting resolved. She told me that she'd experienced the same sense of calmness during the day. Prior to this incident, we prayed together once a week, but not daily. So, we decided to pray together again the next morning. Every morning for the rest of that week, we spent two or three minutes in prayer before I went out the front door. As a result of what God did during those five days, we made a marriage-altering decision to *never* leave the house in the morning without praying together. That was years ago and to this day, praying together remains an integral part of our morning routine.

Making Your Marriage a Prayer Priority

When God first began reconciling our relationship, we were living over 3,000 miles apart on opposite coasts of the United States. In an effort to grow closer despite the miles between us, we decided to pray together over the phone once a week. Every Sunday, we took turns calling each other and sharing prayer requests. Prayer bridged the miles between us in indescribable ways.

When we remarried, we thought it would be wise to keep a good thing going. To this day, we meet together on Sunday nights and share our weekly praises and prayer requests. This gives us the opportunity to check-in with each other regarding any concerns that surface during the week. In addition to sharing our prayer requests, we review the requests from the previous week and discuss the ways God answered our prayers and deepened our relationship. (More information about this weekly prayer and devotional time is discussed in Chapter 10.)

One of the greatest challenges for a couple who gets back together after a crisis, separation, and/or divorce is that there is a tendency to point the finger at their spouse for the changes that need to be made, instead of praying for him/her. I'll never forget the wise piece of advice I (Penny) received from my friend, Annie, just after Clint and I remarried.

"It's not your job to be the Holy Spirit in Clint's life or to try and make him change."

I wish I could say I've always heeded Annie's words, but at the start, I was definitely guilty of trying to improve Clint and of determining the changes I thought he should make to strengthen our marriage. It was not until I realized that praying for, blessing, and affirming Clint would make a far greater impact on our marriage than any changes I might try to force on him.

Over the years that we've been in ministry, I've noticed I'm not alone in the tendency to try and figure out ways to modify my husband. Many people rattle off a litany of things they want to change about their spouses when they come to us for help. As a result of the constant nagging and fault-finding, division has erected walls in these marriages that seem impossible to break down.

Save yourself a lot of heartache. Instead of spending all your energy trying to change your spouse, ask God how He wants to change you, and how *He* wants you to pray for your spouse. Use Scripture to guide you in praying for him/her. In an effort to affirm your spouse in spite of your differences, encourage his/her varied interests, hobbies, and ways of doing things, even if these things frustrate you. Pay close attention to what's important to your mate. Study him/her. Taking a genuine interest in the things that are meaningful to your spouse and faithfully praying for him/her will create new connection points in your relationship. One of the greatest gifts you can give to your husband/wife is the freedom to be different than you. Even if you don't always understand what makes your spouse tick, you can find creative and meaningful ways to demonstrate love.

One very simple and practical way that I pray for Clint is by using one of our wedding photos as my Bible bookmark. On the back of the photo, I place a *Post-it* note which contains a prayer list for him. That way, every day when I open my Bible, I reflect on the priceless gift of being married and remember to pray for Clint. As I sense God answering prayers or making changes, I remove the old *Post-it* and replace it with a new one. Each time I do so, I ask God to show me how *He* sees Clint and how *He* wants me to pray for him.

Another practical way I pray for Clint is to get up before he does and sit in the recliner where he sits when he meets with God. I suppose in a very tangible way, sitting in that special place helps me shift my perspective. When I pray in that chair, I ask God to reveal how I can best support Clint and become a more "suitable" helpmate for him. Sometimes, I'll just place my hand on his Bible or devotional materials, praying as the Spirit leads regarding Clint's personal walk with God. At other times, I'll pray for God to establish, anoint, and bless the projects Clint is working on for our ministry.

One of the most effective and thorough ways I have ever prayed for Clint, our marriage, and my role as his wife was when I put together a prayer scrapbook. On each page of a blank book, I glued a different photo of Clint, or of the two of us. Then, at the top of each page, I wrote down a particular area of concern such as family relationships, physical health, serving God together, spiritual growth, etc. Once the photos were in place on each page, I asked God for a Scripture verse or passage to claim regarding that specific focus area and wrote that verse/passage next to each photo. For well over a year, I used the prayer scrapbook to write down prayer requests and keep track of the way God answered. I also noted the changes God made in Clint's heart and in mine.

As I flip through the pages of that prayer book now, I'm astounded at the ways God responded to my prayers and the changes He made in both of us. That scrapbook has become a treasured memento and some undeniable evidence of the powerful tool that prayer proved to be in restoring our marriage.

Creating a prayer scrapbook for your marriage and/or your family is a great way to rebuild unity and nurture the reconciliation of relationships between family members. It's also a profound way to trace God's hand over your lives as you become more like Him.

Prayer with a Guarantee

During the first two years of our remarriage, we decided to conduct a mini-investigation on the topic and practice of prayer. We each spent time searching the Scriptures during our individual quiet times. In addition, we read books together about prayer and discussed our opinions about what we were reading. At one point, our curiosity grew as to how others organized their prayer lives and whether or not they used lists, journals, or other methods to keep track of prayer requests and God's answers. What we discovered was that there are unlimited ways to approach, organize, and utilize prayer, but what matters most is that we make praying for each other and our marriage a very high priority.

During this same time period, author and pastor, Rick Warren, released his book, *The Purpose Driven Life,*[4] and we committed to participating in the forty-day program our church was emphasizing. This included reading a chapter of Warren's book together each evening. As we sat at the table that first night, we decided it might be a good idea to compose a prayer that we could use to guide us through the forty-day journey we were starting. Penny grabbed a pencil and paper and jotted down our thoughts as we talked. By the end of the evening, we'd composed the following prayer:

Heavenly Father,

We surrender to You day #_____. We surrender ourselves and all the resources You've given us to accomplish Your purpose. Reveal to us Your purpose for our lives and expose the obstacles of sin that keep us from living out that purpose. Lord, release Your power within us to do the right thing; not only with those we love, but those we dislike as well. Help us to be a vessel through which Jesus shines. We surrender our minds, hearts, souls, bodies, and wills to Your sovereign authority. We are Yours, Lord. May we be closer to You by the day's end. In Jesus' name we pray. Amen.

We wrote down that prayer, tucked a copy of it into our Bibles, and committed to praying it every day for forty days. Almost immediately, a dramatic shift occurred in our relationships with God and each other. Neither of us could put our fingers on what was happening, at first. But over time, we realized that the prayer we'd written guaranteed a "yes" response from God. In other words, when we analyzed the prayer, we realized that we hadn't asked God for tangible things, detailed plans, or material possessions as we had so often in the past. Instead, we surrendered all those things to God daily, asking Him to have His way in our hearts. That's when we realized that God will *always* agree to prayers like those!

As a result of the discovery that God would give prayers of this nature His automatic approval, we created a list of simple prayer phrases to use in our marriage. If you're willing to submit yourselves fully to God, we guarantee that, as simple as they may seem, these prayers will be answered with His zealous nod. Ever since we started using these types of prayers, our faith has deepened, our marriage has improved, and God has given us a desire to trust Him with our lives to an even greater degree.

Prayers with a Guarantee

- Please give us Your mind and wisdom so we think like You in every circumstance.
- Reveal Yourself to us through Your Word and show us Your perfect will for our relationship.
- Mold us, shape us, and transform us into Your image.
- Meet us in the midst of this conflict. Show us the tangible ways we can honor You throughout this ordeal.
- Reveal any sins that clutter our minds and hinder our hearts from hearing You or seeing our relationship from Your perspective.
- Change our hearts so that we're more forgiving, merciful, humble, and gentle.
- Surround us with wise counsel, godly support, and opportunities for healthy fellowship.
- Please don't give us anything that will bring us more pleasure than You.

Cutting through Everyday Conflict

Before you were married, did anyone ever sit you down and tell you there would be times of disagreement in your relationship? Most couples we speak to never imagined they'd be at such great odds with each other. It's sobering to consider the high percentage of the couples who sign a marriage certificate, will one day sign the documents to finalize their divorce.

When we were married the first time, we didn't know that we should proactively prepare for conflict. Instead, we were so caught up with being in love and experiencing all the wonderful aspects of the honeymoon phase of our relationship, we didn't know what to do when we hit our first major disagreement. Neither of us had ever seen conflict play out in a healthy way between a husband and wife. So out of ignorance, instead of managing our problems with God's help, we reacted and responded to each other out of our own emotions, opinions, and selfishness. Our priorities were all about getting our own needs met and not about serving each other. We became a part of the very statistic that we're now so passionate about reducing.

Back then, it never occurred to us to use prayer as a power tool to work through our differences. This time around, we know better than to repeat past mistakes. At first, we weren't exactly sure how to approach making a change in this area. With time and practice, however, we discovered that *immediately* calling on God as our Advocate and Judge had to be our *first* line of defense against division. Many times since then, one of us has stopped right in the middle of a disagreement and prayed something like, "Lord, help us! We're struggling and we need Your wisdom and opinion. Meet us in the middle of this conflict and show us a better way."

At other times, we've excused ourselves from a conversation that seemed to be turning sour in order to go into another room and pray alone for a while. Through these kinds of experiences, we've realized that when we include God and seek His righteousness and wisdom through prayer, He consistently settles our disputes long before things get out of hand.

While Penny and I share many similarities and common interests, we are two very different people. When we speak to couples at conferences and seminars, we explain our differences by stating that Penny is a psalm and I am a proverb. Penny is expressive and a true visionary who thrives best when she's thrown by the seat of her pants into a challenging situation. I am a linear thinker and operate best when there's a plan laid out or a specific model to follow. These differences definitely make our marriage interesting as well as challenging.

After *many* opportunities to practice handling our differences more appropriately through prayer, we created a simple diagram to help other couples prayerfully approach and resolve their differences. When combined with prayer, the *Gradients of Agreement* diagram will help you negotiate with each other when you don't see eye-to-eye. That way, you can maintain peace and harmony in your home, despite your unique personalities and differences.

Gradients of Agreement

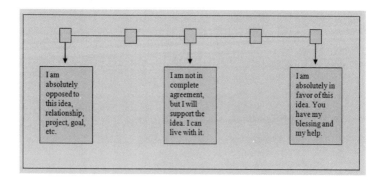

I am absolutely opposed to this idea, relationship, project, goal, etc.

I am not in complete agreement, but I will support the idea. I can live with it.

I am absolutely in favor of this idea. You have my blessing and my help.

Think of this diagram as a visual tool you carry in your mind to help you clarify where you are on the gradient scale when a disagreement is brewing. If used prayerfully, this diagram can help you clarify and express your thoughts, opinions, and feelings. Here are some general tips and guidelines we've developed in relation to using the *Gradients of Agreement* diagram in order to bring clarity and to help resolve conflict.

- If you find yourselves at opposite ends of the gradient, stop the conversation, pray, and cool off. Set another time to restart the discussion, after both of you have had the chance to pray on your own and to figure out why you feel the way you do. This will give God the opportunity to change *your* heart and allow you to gain some perspective.

- The diagram and your disagreement work in conjunction with your individual time with God. In other words, it's much easier for your spouse to trust your ideas and opinions when he/she knows you're seeking God's counsel and wisdom every day by spending time in His Word.

- If one of you is completely opposed to an idea, project, relationship, decision, purchase, etc., that your spouse still feels strongly about, wait, pray, and seek God together through His Word. Ask God to use the Holy Spirit, the Bible, wise counsel, and each other to confirm whether or not you should move forward. Mutually submit to God and to one another. Don't forge ahead unless you both feel that God has said to do so and you are fairly close together on the gradient scale.

- If you are in the "I can live with it" box regarding something your spouse is proposing, discuss the kinds of support you will give to him/her. It's never fair to harden your heart and pull away from your spouse because you aren't in *absolute* agreement with him/her. Be clear and specific about your concerns, but be willing to assist your spouse. Remember, you're called to serve one another and put your spouse's needs above your own, even when you might not understand him/her.

- Even when you're both in full agreement, you must be certain that God is in favor of what you want to do. This process takes time and prayer. You should never let impulsivity prematurely move you ahead of God or lead you outside His will.

- Sometimes, it's helpful to bring tough conflicts before a prayer/accountability partner for wise counsel.

- God will often use your spouse to confirm the direction of an idea, project, goal, etc. Be open to having God speak to you *through* your spouse. This will take practice, patience, and trust.

- Always be open to a change of heart. God alone can change the hearts and minds of His people. Through prayer, place your frustration, hope, and spouse into God's hands and, as stated before, keep asking Him how He wants to change *your* heart.

If your disagreements are handled in a way that honors God, every single one of them can be used for His glory and to strengthen your marriage. If God truly is an integral part of your union, then He must be invited to participate in your disagreements and He must be given a say in what transpires. When allowed to intervene, the Holy Spirit will absorb all the excess energy, pressure, tension, and stress so often involved in conflict resolution. When you are quick to allow prayer to help you cut through conflict, you open the door for God to enter in and change everything.

Nehemiah's impulsivity to pray through every challenge set a high standard in your ongoing work to remain reconciled. Bailing out of the rebuilding project was not an option for Nehemiah and walking out on your marriage isn't an option for you. No matter what transpires, it's never appropriate to dangle threats of separation or divorce over one another during conflict. Whether you're angry, confused, weak, tired, frustrated, discouraged, or doubtful, looking for a way out isn't the answer. Instead, exercise your option to pray. If we, as husbands and wives, have any impulses during the restoration process, let us be impulsive to pray immediately, fervently, frequently, and honestly.

Chuck and Micki Ann have learned a thing or two about using prayer to cut through conflict and draw them closer together. Having started the process of marital restoration many years ago, they developed a simple non-verbal cue that serves as an immediate call to prayer. All one spouse has to do is hold out his/her hand palm up toward the other, and all conversation or activity is ceased. Immediately, they join hands and begin to pray.

When we interviewed them about the role of prayer in their marriage and family, Chuck made the following statement that has stuck with us ever since. "It's not so much that prayer automatically changes the nature of our circumstances. But, more importantly, prayer humbles and changes *my* heart toward the circumstance."

As we've gotten to know this couple over the years, we've also seen how they've trained up their children in the way of prayer. As a matter of fact, intercession has become such an integral piece of the fabric that makes up this family that they dedicated one entire room in their house as a special place for prayer. Clint and I had the privilege of assisting in the construction of this *prayer house* and were greatly inspired by the need, desire, and passion for prayer to encompass *every* aspect of this family's life. Intercession is as paramount to their survival each day as is bread and water. This is how it should be!

Severing Your Strongholds

One of the challenges of restoring your relationship is dealing with conflicts from the past which may unexpectedly revisit your marriage. In the next chapter, we'll discuss this in more detail, but for the purposes of this chapter, we must note an important point. Deeply rooted strongholds are often at the source of our unbecoming behaviors and choices. Prayer is the power tool that can slice through these strongholds so they are no longer a source of division.

An elementary definition of a stronghold is *an unhealthy or skewed pattern of thinking or relating that is based on deception.* Anything having to do with deception is always a direct weapon Satan wields against God's people. However, God has given us a weapon that can obliterate *all* strongholds.

For though we live in the world, we do not wage war as the world does. The weapons we fight with are not the weapons of the world. On the contrary, they have divine power to demolish strongholds. We demolish arguments and every pretension that sets itself up against the knowledge of God, and we take captive every thought to make it obedient to Christ.

2 Corinthians 10:3–5

Strongholds cause us to think and act in ways that divert us away from experiencing true wholeness in Christ and keep us from receiving God's full measure of blessing. Strongholds can also make our relationships with God and others grow stagnant because they're based on faulty reasoning and false arguments. For example, many people admit to viewing God as a tyrannical ruler who only exists to angrily hand down punishment. As a result, they get stuck living with a sense of guilt or shame that hovers over their lives, keeping them from fully experiencing God's grace and love.

In marriage, a stronghold often masquerades itself as a repeat offense. Repeat offenses tend to occur in every marriage, but they pose an even greater threat to couples working through the process of restoration. What we've discovered over time is that when a problem or issue repeatedly resurfaces between us, there is likely an underlying stronghold at work and it takes us a while to unmask it. Strongholds are hidden far beneath the surface of ongoing conflict because the Enemy does not want his deceptive tactics to be exposed. Prayer is the critical element in accurately identifying and slaying every stronghold.

There isn't a more appropriate saved marriage story to illustrate this point than that of Pastor Joe and Gerri Begay, who are Native American and were raised on the Navajo Reservation in Arizona. We first met Joe and Gerri after one of our speaking engagements in Farmington, New Mexico.

"Joe and I got married before I finished high school," explained Gerri. "After four kids, years of repeated rage, and Joe's addiction to alcohol, we got divorced. For the sake of our children, we eventually reconciled and remarried after having our fifth child. However, when we hit conflict again we brought up offenses from the past. After our second divorce, I lost hope. I started leaving my children and hanging out at the border town bars."

Joe continued their story.

"It was after the failure of our second marriage that we individually invited Christ to end our addictions to alcohol and to stop all the other repeat offenses that had torn us apart in the past. We vowed to each other that we would never, never bring up past offenses again. At the altar of a local church, Gerri and I got on our knees and asked God to take over control of our lives."

Shortly thereafter, Joe and Gerri remarried for the third (and final) time.

"We are living proof," said Joe, "that the way to victory over alcohol, bitterness, and hatred is through Jesus Christ."[5]

Today, Joe and Gerri pastor a thriving church in Chinle, AZ. During our time with them, they told us about how the strongholds of alcohol, drugs, and gambling are spreading across the Navajo Nation. To help others find freedom from repeat offenses, strongholds, and addictions, Pastor Joe and Gerri make themselves available for a time of open prayer ministry after each worship service. We were humbled to witness them in action when we visited their church during a 40-Day Marriage Mission Trip. It was very plain to see why they plan on spending the rest of their lives leading others to victory in Christ through prayer.

Getting Specific with God

In her book, *Prayer Essentials for Living in His Presence,* author Sylvia Gunter writes, "Every family needs some measure of release from generational bondages. Maybe we have never thought about how we pass down from generation to generation a family stronghold or altar at which we bow down. Think about evidences of family shrines: 'The Smiths always…' or 'The Smiths are sixth generation…' Or perhaps a bondage exists to a behavior that repeats itself generation after generation, for example, anger, sexual sin, or alcoholism." The author goes on to state that the cycle of generational strongholds can be broken through prayer and that it is essential to also ask God to establish new lines of blessing for the coming generations in your family line.[6]

Being set free from strongholds will require you to get specific with God. One of the tools we teach couples in our seminars is how to write prayers together that are specifically focused on stopping the cycle of repeat offenses and shattering strongholds. We realize that the Holy Spirit can break a stronghold immediately. We've seen it happen. However, based on our experiences, we also know that there are some strongholds that involve employing a *process of prayer* to stop their destructive cycle. Specifically, we testify to the fact that writing prayers together and praying fervently can sever some strongholds more effectively and permanently than anything else you might attempt.

Simply stated, when a couple comes up against the same issue in their marriage over and over again, we suggest that they join together to compose a prayer specifically tailored to identify the stronghold, expose it, and tear it down. To help you better understand this process, we've written a step-by-step guide and a

103

sample prayer that focuses on breaking a stronghold many marriages are facing today: money.

Let's assume you and your spouse have recurring arguments over money. Oftentimes this stronghold will manifest itself in repeated offenses over things like spending/saving habits, budgets, lack of adequate financial resources, impulsive purchases, or inconsistent tithing, to name a few. These things may even be traced back through several generations. Based on this assumption, let this step-by-step guide help you grasp the concept of using prayer as a power tool to tear down strongholds.

- **Step One:** Ask the Holy Spirit to expose the true nature of the stronghold. Don't try to discuss the issue or write a prayer without first asking God to reveal the real root of it. This process may take some time. Bring the stronghold and its manifestation (the repeated offenses or issues) to God together and ask Him to shed His light and truth on it. Locate a verse or passage of Scripture to claim over this problem and use it to help you compose a prayer together.

- **Step Two:** Take turns contributing ideas, words, and sentences to form a prayer that expresses both of your hearts. The prayer should focus on tearing down the stronghold *and* replacing your unhealthy thinking patterns and/or behaviors with godly attitudes and actions. It is essential to replace unhealthy thinking and behavior with godly actions and attitudes so as not to fill that void with another stronghold.

- **Step Three:** After you write the prayer, make copies of it and post it in several places (home, office, mirror, car, journal, Bible, and so forth) as a reminder to pray it regularly, with a believing heart. Be patient. Because some strongholds can be traced back several generations, it may take some time to completely uproot and destroy it.

- **Step Four:** Pray until. In other words, keep praying, asking, seeking, and knocking on God's door until the stronghold is removed and you experience a change in the dynamics of your relationship with Him and each other. You may sense this liberation and deliverance immediately, or over time. Remember that God's timelines and processes are just as important as the outcomes, especially when it comes to changes of heart, attitude, and action.

- **Step Five:** Throughout the process, rejoice and give thanks for all the ways God answers your prayer, tears down the stronghold, and gives you victory. Observe the way He works and praise Him for new thoughts and behavior patterns that are grounded in the Word.

The following is a sample prayer that was written based on the step-by-step process outlined here. If you are currently living in bondage to the stronghold of money, you're welcome to use this prayer. However, we also want to encourage you to ask the Holy Spirit for His guidance in composting a prayer that addresses your specific behavior patterns and the ways in which these things need to be exposed and uprooted.

Sample Prayer to Break the Stronghold of Money

Holy Spirit, You've revealed to us that our repeated arguments over money are really a deeply-rooted stronghold. Luke 16:13 says, "No servant can serve two masters. Either he will hate the one and love the other, or he will be devoted to one and despise the other. You cannot serve both God and Money."

Our marriage has been a slave to money. We confess our sins of unhealthy thinking and behavior to You and we ask for Your forgiveness and cleansing. We specifically ask, in Jesus' name, that You completely sever the stronghold of money in our marriage and grant us freedom from what has bound us and kept us from experiencing more of Your blessing. Please break the ties of this stronghold over past and future generations. Set our family free from living under the impact and bondage of deception. Replace our ungodly thoughts and actions with those that respect You and edify each other. Guide us to answers in Your Word so we honor You with the funds You've given us. Show us Your better way of dealing with every area of our finances, including the faithful giving of tithes and offerings that belong to You. Temper our impulsive purchases. Show us biblical, wise, and tangible ways to save, spend, and share these resources. Please provide for the needs of our family and enable us to become faithful stewards. Help us strike a balance and blend our differences together so that we come into a financial agreement that is not our plan, but Your plan. In Jesus' name. Amen.

Rebuilding Intimacy through Prayer

We would be extremely remiss if we didn't discuss the vital role of prayer in restoring and rebuilding physical and emotional intimacy in your marriage. Most couples who've been through a crisis, separation, and/or divorce are starting from scratch in all facets of marital intimacy. That was certainly the case for us. Intimacy was grossly lacking in our first marriage and, due to what transpired at the end of it, we were definitely starting at zero when we remarried.

I vividly recall the anxiety I felt about developing physical intimacy with Clint. There is no pretty way to put it. Even though neither of us had remarried during the years we wandered from God, we'd both crossed over appropriate physical/sexual boundaries with others. While we asked Him to forgive us for these sins and fully disclosed this information to each other, we had no idea how all this would play out in our remarriage.

Many couples we serve in ministry today are facing the very same scenario. Often times, infidelity, sexual addiction, or other sins have occurred outside of marriage and these indiscretions threaten to dash all hopes for healing. However, when we share our testimony across the nation, we tell couples that if God healed all the mistakes and pain from *our* pasts, He is willing and able do the same thing for them. God longs for the chance to restore the past and bring wholeness to your marriage. Redeeming *every* part of our sinfulness and brokenness is the reason Jesus came to earth. For the purposes of this chapter, let us give you a concrete example of how prayer helped us over the intimacy hurdle.

Due to the details involved in our reconciliation, Clint only had about eight weeks to put his home up for sale in Florida, pack his belongings, and drive over 3,000 miles to get to California in time for our wedding. So, not only was there an eleven-year gap in our relationship, and indiscretions in our pasts, but we didn't get to spend time together until just five days before we remarried. Although there were few opportunities to begin building intimacy prior to our remarriage, we firmly relied on God for what seemed impossible.

Three days before our wedding, we invited our marriage mentors, Dale and Colleen, to come over to what would soon be our home together as husband and wife. Our plan was to have them cleanse and bless each room of the house, believing with us that prayer would be the catalyst to create, establish, and nurture intimacy there. The four of us spent the evening walking from room to room, cleansing and blessing each area. In the living room, we prayed for things like fellowship and times of rest. In the kitchen, we prayed about our health and the breaking of bread together. In the bathrooms, we prayed for our image to mirror the image of Christ. On the front porch, we prayed for protection in all our coming and going and for nothing divisive to ever enter our marriage or home. This time of prayer continued throughout each room of the house, as well as the front and backyard.

When we all walked into the master bedroom, I felt a lump forming in my throat. Tears of fear and anxiety welled up in my eyes and spilled down my cheeks. But, with the four of us kneeling together at the bedside, we prayed fervently for the establishment of sexual and emotional intimacy. We prayed for cleansing from the past and complete healing for our future. It was a time Clint and I will always treasure and we're convinced that the prayers the four of us offered to God that night continue to be answered to this day.

Not only do we highly advocate prayer as the backbone for re-establishing intimacy at the start of your restoration, but praying for emotional, physical, and spiritual intimacy should become a regular part of your marriage prayer life and mustn't be neglected at any time during the remainder of your lives together.

Allow us to be quite frank here. Prayer should be a part of *everything* you do. For example, have you ever considered praying about the sexual part of your marriage? Have you asked God to show you how to be physically intimate? Have you prayed that your times of sexual intimacy would reflect His perfect and holy design for marriage? Have you prayed prior to and/or after making love?

Some couples don't feel comfortable praying these kinds of prayers together or aloud, at first. That's understandable. If that's the case for you, pray silently on your own. It doesn't matter *how* you pray. It matters *that* you pray and believe God is able to completely restore intimacy in all the facets of your marriage. If you're uncertain as to how to begin the process of praying through this vital area of your marriage, we've written a few prayer starters to assist you.

Sample Prayers for Intimacy

- Erase any prior images or memories that are a consequence of sin.
- Increase our desire and passion for each other.
- Heal the areas of insecurity and vulnerability in us.

Continued on the next page…

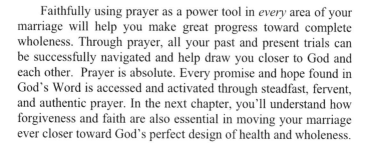

Sample Prayers for Intimacy

- Show us how to please one another and to be sensitive to each other's needs.
- Cleanse us from the sinful ways we damaged intimacy and rebuild it into our marriage.
- Restore and protect the fidelity in our marriage and let no one/nothing come between us.
- Teach us how to know and respect the areas of insecurity and vulnerability when it comes to each other's self-image and sexuality.
- Enable us to communicate our emotional and physical needs without the fear of rejection.
- Give us the words to affirm each other's inward and outward beauty.

Faithfully using prayer as a power tool in *every* area of your marriage will help you make great progress toward complete wholeness. Through prayer, all your past and present trials can be successfully navigated and help draw you closer to God and each other. Prayer is absolute. Every promise and hope found in God's Word is accessed and activated through steadfast, fervent, and authentic prayer. In the next chapter, you'll understand how forgiveness and faith are also essential in moving your marriage ever closer toward God's perfect design of health and wholeness.

CHAPTER EXERCISES

Establishing a Prayerful Marriage

Lord, teach us to faithfully pray for our marriage and each other. Show us the ways we can integrate powerful, effective, and restorative prayer into our relationship. We believe prayer is an important key to our complete healing. Use Your Holy Spirit to remind us to pray together about *everything* in our lives. Teach us how to seek Your presence and make Your eternal priorities our own. Prepare and equip us for times of disagreement. We desire to handle conflict in a way that pleases You and strengthens our relationship. Broaden our perspective during disagreements so that we see more than just our own needs, wants, and desires. Bless us with what You know we are lacking. Please show us creative and fresh ways to develop and deepen emotional, physical, and spiritual intimacy. Grant us the wisdom to expose and sever the strongholds that hinder us. Pardon all our sins and shortcomings and grant us the mercy to forgive each other without condition. Cover our relationship with Your sovereign hand of protection from any attempts the Enemy might make to divide us or break up our family. We ask all these things of You in faith, believing that You will hear our prayers and respond. In Jesus' name we pray. Amen.

Write a Prayer

Think about a repeat offense in your marriage. Ask God to reveal the underlying stronghold and apply the steps outlined in this chapter to compose a prayer together. Your goal is to expose and tear down the stronghold that is hindering you. Take turns offering ideas, words, and sentences until you have written a prayer that reflects both of your hearts. Pray until.

Scripture Reading

Review Nehemiah 1 and read Nehemiah 9 before answering the following questions.

Questions to Consider

1. What are some of the ideas about prayer in this chapter and/or in the book of Nehemiah that spark your interest?

2. What/who is hindering you from spending more time in prayer individually and with your spouse? How can you remedy this?

3. What do you notice about the confession of sin recorded in Nehemiah 1 and 9?

4. Consider the chapters of Nehemiah that you've read thus far. Is there any evidence of generational strongholds? If so, what are they?

5. Take out your marriage timeline. How might prayer have positively impacted the negative life events you've listed on the timeline thus far?

At the beginning of our crisis, old triggers would come minute-by-minute. Now, they only happen a few times a year, at the most. We've learned that when a trigger comes we must keep our armor on (Ephesians 6:11) and hold every thought captive to the obedience of Christ (2 Corinthians 10:5).

Individually, we immediately pray about trigger thoughts when they come and lay them at the foot of the cross realizing they're usually just based on fear that seeks to steal, kill and destroy. Usually the thought is crushed immediately by God's truth, but if it lingers, we share it with each other and pray about it together. We still work on not getting offended by one another's worries, fears or negative thoughts and not allowing triggers to take us back to the guilt and shame of our past.

Love is a risk, but we've decided it's a risk worth taking. We've removed the word 'divorce' from our vocabulary and committed to investing time and effort to grow together, instead of apart. Each day, our energies are put into fighting for our marriage and in building a legacy for our children.

Continued on the next page…

Continued from the previous page…

The *only* place to begin forgiving each other is with Christ. Invite God into your struggle and ask Him for help. Work on growing in your relationship with God individually and as a couple. Work on forgiving your spouse and asking forgiveness for your part in the offense. This is a critical step in reconciliation. Jesus tells us to forgive as He has forgiven us. Never forget your marriage is worth saving; God has a beautiful and newly-designed relationship just for you, if you lean in and follow His path!

Dick and Joni Boyle
AMFM Marriage Ambassadors
Puyallup, WA

Chapter 6 – Building Bridges of Forgiveness and Faith

As marriage missionaries, Penny and I travel across the United States sharing our testimony of reconciliation on 40-Day Marriage Mission Trips. While we don't often get the time or opportunity to go into lengthy detail as to the specific nature of our break-up, Penny does share that she was unfaithful at the end of our first marriage, and I admit the ways my tough-guy personality contributed to our divorce. After our speaking engagements, I'm always surprised by the number of men who approach me and ask, "Clint, how could you ever forgive Penny for what she did?" Sometimes they'll go on to tell me their wives had an affair too, or did something else they consider, "absolutely unforgivable."

My response to these guys is always the same. "How could I *not* forgive Penny?" If they stick around long enough to let me finish, I explain that, during the years we were apart, I finally came to a true understanding of the fact that although I'm entitled to nothing, Christ forgave me of *all* my sins and He asks me to do the same where others are concerned. That included forgiving Penny. When I first accepted Christ as my Savior in 1981, I knew about His forgiveness, but it wasn't until many years later that I really understood the magnitude of what He did on the Cross to pardon my sins. I also remind these men that although I wasn't unfaithful to Penny in our marriage there were still many things I'd done wrong and that I needed to ask Penny's forgiveness for those things, just like she did with me.

The truth is, I forgave Penny a long time before I ever received her letter asking me for forgiveness. But, what I did was nothing noble. Forgiveness is part of the cross we're to bear as Christ's disciples. It is our obligation to make every effort to pursue and extend forgiveness, no matter what the offense or the cost.

For the most part, we've noticed that women tend to be less reluctant than men when it comes to saying, "I'm sorry. Will you please forgive me?" Guys, it's time to make a change. I encourage you to take the lead when it comes to getting your marriage back in step. Taking the initiative and apologizing when conflicts arise is your spiritual responsibility. If you want your wives to respect your leadership, you must nurture their respect by being man enough to say, "I'm sorry for my part of the problem. Will you forgive me?" Nothing will melt the tension in your marriage faster than apologizing and humbly asking for forgiveness.

Nehemiah perfectly reflects the point I'm trying to stress. He was willing to take full responsibility for acknowledging and identifying himself as a part of the problem during his attempts to reform the Israelites and rebuild Jerusalem.

I confess the sins we Israelites, including myself and my father's house, have committed against you. We have acted very wickedly toward you. We have not obeyed the commands, decrees and laws you gave your servant Moses.

Nehemiah 1:6–7

Nehemiah wasn't quick to point the finger at others as he petitioned God. Instead, he admitted his sinful nature as a part of what needed redemption. "*We* have acted very wickedly" and "*we* have not obeyed," are the words he stated as he stood before God (emphasis added). Nehemiah was also aware of the wicked acts that had been committed against God in past generations and he wasn't hesitant to take responsibility by privately and publicly confessing the sins of his forefathers. The sin from past generations can subtly permeate the lineage of a family for years without being disclosed. It lurks under the radar of our everyday awareness like an undetected poison, giving off toxins that target our spiritual freedom.

As far as I'm concerned, we can't engage in times of confession and repentance often enough. Honest confession and repentance of your shortcomings is an ongoing part of nurturing a *culture* of forgiveness and reconciliation that permeates all of your relationships. Many of the problems in marriages today are a result of pride and an unwillingness to own up to mistakes and sins, both past and present.

What's the Difference?

The focus of this chapter is to learn how combining forgiveness and faith can build bridges of reconciliation over the problems of your past. Before we proceed, however, let's be clear about the difference between *forgiveness* and *reconciliation*. The simplest explanation is this: It only takes one party to *forgive* an offense or to ask someone for forgiveness, but it takes two parties to *reconcile* a relationship. For example, I forgave Penny on my own, but our marriage wasn't reconciled until we *both* came together and made the decision to re-establish our relationship.

As stated in an earlier chapter, Webster's dictionary defines the word *reconciliation* as *bringing together again in love, re-establishing a friendship, or reaching a compromise or agreement about your differences or opposing views.* During His ministry on earth, Jesus modeled forgiveness and reconciliation in numerous ways. You can see examples of Jesus' actions throughout the four Gospels as He responded to relationships in crisis. Unfortunately, the ways of the world run in direct opposition to forgiveness and the reconciliation of relationships. Satan loves nothing more than to drive a wedge between believers. He primarily does this through unforgiveness, which breaks down relationships more swiftly than anything else.

Couples who've initially passed through a crisis must constantly be aware of the subtle ways the Enemy will attempt to divert them away from a closer relationship with God and each other by harboring unforgiveness. Immediately after we remarried, Penny and I experienced the Enemy's desire to use what had happened in our pasts to divide and conquer us. His first assault came on our wedding day.

Our ceremony and reception in 2002 were incredible. We were surrounded by family, friends, and colleagues. Even some of the people who were present at our first wedding came to celebrate with us. Penny was beside herself with joy the entire night. That's not to say that I wasn't, but most of the people at our wedding were much more important in her life during our years apart because I'd moved away to Florida and lost touch. Naturally, Penny wanted to spend as much time with her family and friends as possible. But, like most guys, I had other things on my mind. After a few hours of celebrating, I was ready to begin our first night together after eleven long years apart. But, it seemed the more ready I was to go, the more content Penny was to stay. As I observed her celebrating with friends and colleagues—people I was only briefly acquainted with—one of her friends from church walked up to me, leaned in front of my face, and said, "Hey bud, make sure you don't mess this up."

I just smiled and nodded at the guy, but inside, anger was brewing. After all, we had only been married a few hours and I didn't need that kind of pressure. While I didn't realize what was happening at the time, I now understand that I was not only feeling the stress from the present, but something had triggered failure from the past as well.

I was ready to be alone with Penny, but it seemed like it took her forever to say all her goodbyes. Even then, I knew that if she'd had her way, we would have stayed at the reception for a few more hours. The words of caution from her friend burned inside me, but I didn't tell Penny how I was feeling. When we finally got in the car, the tension had mounted. We exchanged very few words on the drive back to the house.

By the grace of God, we managed to overcome this problem and enjoy our first night back together as husband and wife. But, after this experience, we both realized that dealing rationally and appropriately with these kinds of painful memories from the past (as well as new challenges in the present) would take some serious effort.

Later, we discussed what happened and during our conversation, I discovered that Penny was having her own upsurge of pain from the past. She explained the ways she felt I was subtly trying to control her by being silent, yet visibly aggravated when she wanted to stay at the reception, and I wanted to leave. For Penny, my attitude stirred up old memories of the conflicts that occurred at the end of our first marriage when I shut down and stopped communicating with her.

Building Bridges over Unpleasant Memories

We now refer to these uncomfortable experiences as *traumatic triggers*: unpleasant memories that unexpectedly surface and suck the life out of your relationship. All the couples we've worked with over the years admit to experiencing these moments and, no doubt, you will too (if you haven't already). The way you handle these triggers can make or break your relationship. The couples we've served say the same thing and we wholeheartedly agree: When painful or fearful memories from the past are triggered, it feels as though someone is sucking the breath from your chest like a high-powered vacuum.

These rushes of pain and fear are ripe with the potential to have unforgiveness subtly creep in and drive a wedge between you in nothing flat. Therefore, it's important to recognize these kinds of events while they're happening and to pray for healthy ways to deal with them. We like to use a visual image to help couples understand traumatic triggers and the ways in which they can proactively and effectively use these experiences to draw closer together.

Imagine you and your spouse are standing at the bank of a swiftly rushing river. The river represents the pain, dissention, fear, betrayal, and other sins from the past. The waters appear dark, murky, and impossible to cross. If you attempt to wade through the river, you're certain you'll be swept up in the current, sucked under, and drown. However, you also know that you have to get to the other side of the river to continue your journey together. You need a bridge to stretch over these treacherous waters.

Forgiveness and faith are your bridge builders. Combined with prayer, forgiveness and faith are the only things that will build a bridge strong enough to safely carry you to the other side.

When a painful event or memory in your relationship is triggered, you must recognize what is happening, forgive the offense, and take a step of faith (whatever that looks like at the time). Sometimes, asking God and your spouse for forgiveness turns out to be greatest step of faith required to get over the triggered memory. And sometimes, extending forgiveness to your spouse (or someone else) is the faith God requires.

Nehemiah stood on the banks of some pretty murky waters himself and he needed a very sturdy bridge to get to the other side. While the first seven chapters of Nehemiah focus on rebuilding the wall around Jerusalem, the last six chapters focus on reform; namely the transformation of Israel's painful past into a promising future. Generations of sin and rebellion, such as pride and idolatry, had ravaged the nation and almost swept them off the map.

> *But they, our forefathers, became arrogant and stiff-necked, and did not obey your commands. They refused to listen and failed to remember the miracles you performed among them. They became stiff-necked and in their rebellion appointed a leader in order to return to their slavery.*
>
> Nehemiah 9:16–17

While he was very aware of the past sins of his forefathers, Nehemiah also knew how to build a bridge with forgiveness and faith. He recognized that God had (and still has) quite a history of building bridges.

But you are a forgiving God, gracious and compassionate; slow to anger and abounding in love. Therefore you did not desert them, even when they cast for themselves an image of a calf and said, "This is your god, who brought you up out of Egypt," or when they committed awful blasphemies.

Nehemiah 9:17–18

While traumatic triggers may seem like an unfortunate by-product of the past, they can be overcome completely, through forgiveness and faith. In addition, these experiences can serve as a catalyst for a stronger relationship. Effectively dealing with traumatic triggers is an ongoing process that takes practice. Over time, you will also realize that part of the benefit of building bridges together is that they allow your perspective on the past to change, in the same way that it shifts when you stand on a bridge and look down. From a higher vantage point, you can look more objectively and clearly at your surroundings and circumstances and together, rise above the very things that took your marriage down in the first place.

Let us give you a specific example of building bridges of forgiveness and faith by introducing you to a couple we met several years ago. When we first saw Scott and Sylvia together, we were taken in by the affectionate demeanor between them. What we didn't realize at the time was that they were barely on the other side of a major crisis. Once we had the opportunity to get to know them a little better, they entrusted their marriage story to us. We could sense their pain as they shared about the traumatic triggers they were experiencing and how those moments seemed to be hindering their progress toward healing.

"It seems like every time I turn around," shared Sylvia, "I'm faced with another memory of what happened and I immediately feel bitter toward Scott."

122

"Frankly, I don't know what to do when this happens," admitted Scott. "I can see the bitterness come over Sylvia and, once again, I'm full of remorse and shame because I know my actions hurt her...and are still hurting her."

Over the next several months, we met with Scott and Sylvia over dinner and talked about the difficulties they were experiencing. We noticed that as a result of their commitment to remain reconciled and to deepen their individual relationships with God, they began taking *every* traumatic trigger to the foot of the cross together, no matter how painful. They intentionally pursued seeking and extending forgiveness and asked God for the faith to move forward over these things. In addition, they each asked Him that key question when something triggered pain from the past: "God, how do You want to change *my* heart through this?"

The Heart of Reconciliation

No matter who is responsible for what transpired in your marriage, God wants to work in *your* heart. People will approach us after we share our testimony wanting to know exactly *how* to reconcile with their spouses. What we try to explain to these folks is that it's much more about the heart.

God wants to make a change in your heart and appropriately handling a traumatic trigger is one of the most effective ways He will accomplish this. You must agree to let God help you foster a spirit of reconciliation and forgiveness in your heart, especially if your spouse has committed offenses that continue to threaten faith's forward motion.

There are ten heart attitudes that will help you build sturdy bridges of forgiveness and faith in your marriage and help you let go of the past. Cultivating these attitudes will lead you to freedom. They will also serve as the support structure for the new bridges of faith you will build together. Each attitude is of equal importance.

1. Be Humble – Humility is often a necessary prerequisite for extending and receiving forgiveness. It indicates that you have an accurate view of who God is, who you are, and who you are becoming. Humility requires complete honesty. It's never easy to admit your mistakes or secrets, but humility and honesty often stimulate mercy. Dancing around the subject because of pride or dishonesty may save face for the moment, but it will also hinder true healing.

2. Be Prayerful – Spend as much time as possible in prayer regarding the traumatic triggers in your marriage. Conflict often arises from these experiences when you point the finger at your spouse's faults or use things from the past against him/her. Instead, direct your hands and heart to God in worship and prayer. If necessary, find a confidential prayer partner who will support you. (More information about prayer partners is included in Chapter 10.) When you sense that a traumatic trigger is occurring, immediately reach out to your spouse and pray together instead of pulling away.

3. Be Careful – Avoid making assumptions or judgments about your spouse's motives, intentions, attitudes, or behaviors. Ask God to reveal any ways in which *you* are setting up roadblocks to reconciliation and/or harboring unforgiveness. Choose appropriate times to discuss traumatic triggers (not late at night, when others are present, or in the heat of the moment). Your spouse is precious to God. Treat his/her feelings and fears with respect and dignity, even if you don't understand them.

4. Be Mindful – Fostering and maintaining a healthy marriage requires a conscious choice to cultivate a mindset of loyalty and devotion *amidst* turbulent waters. We'll be quite frank here. Sometimes when a relationship is not satisfying, it's tempting to seek pleasure elsewhere. No matter how you might *feel*, the arms of another person, spending large sums of money, drinking excessively, indulging in pornography, or confiding in a person of the opposite sex will not bring you lasting satisfaction; not to mention that those things are not safe, moral, or biblical. Make a conscious decision to remain faithful to God, your spouse, and your family in all areas of your life. Spend your time wisely by coping with difficulties in healthy and biblical ways.

5. Be Practical – Make the most of every opportunity to practice, pursue, and seek forgiveness. Ask God to give you practical passages of Scripture to use in order to overcome each traumatic trigger. Write the passages into prayers and use them regularly. When you're hurt, discouraged, or frustrated, get those Scripture passages out and read them aloud to God. Spend some time writing down your feelings, fears, and thoughts in a journal.

6. Be Grateful – Praising and worshiping God in the midst of the pain refocuses your attention on Him and ushers true healing into your heart and mind. Go out of your way to extend gratitude to your spouse. Instead of focusing on your frustration, engage in a labor of love and service for him/her. Worship God with your hands up. Wait for God with your hands open. And, work for God with your hands out.

7. Be Approachable – Let down your defenses. Encourage your spouse to come to you when he/she encounters a traumatic trigger. Be open to hearing your spouse's opinions and feelings. Value the pain and emotion he/she is experiencing by listening and asking clarifying questions. Listen more. Talk less. Welcome the expression of his/her feelings, as difficult as it may be to hear these things. Be aware of your body language at all times. Suspend judgment. Extend mercy.

8. Be Resourceful – If necessary, know when and where to get extra help to deal with the offenses from your past. Sometimes it's advisable to seek out additional resources and support to get you over a particular hurdle. Utilize the wisdom and counsel of other Christians, mentors, pastors, counselors, support providers, health care professionals, or other couples who have come through a crisis. Seek advice and mentoring from a couple who has been through the fire and come out of it stronger. (A list of marriage and family resources can be found in the back of the book.)

9. Be Respectful – Respect and honor the process and timing God is using in your marriage, even though it may feel uncomfortable. Every relationship is different and so is every traumatic trigger. Remember, the way God heals one issue, experience, or relationship may differ from the way He heals another. God is both creative *and* logical. Respect His sovereignty in every situation. Be flexible, open to change, and willing to try new things, even if they seem a little outside of your comfort zone. God can do amazing things with a heart that is willing, submitted, forgiving, and obedient.

10. Be Hopeful – No matter how much murky water has passed under the bridge, there is no brokenness that lies beyond God's restorative reach. When you put your hope in Him, He will always provide a way for you to build a bridge of forgiveness so that, in faith, you can cross over to the other side. He is a God of second chances.

Different Bridges, Same Outcome

As we travel during our mission trips, we drive over many different kinds of bridges. Depending upon the size of the gap spanned by the bridge, the time period when it was constructed, the geographical location and terrain, and the materials used, the bridges we cross *appear* different, but they all serve the same purpose; to get from one side of a chasm to the other. The same holds true for your marriage. At times, because of the nature and consequences of the sins committed, it takes a longer time to build some bridges of forgiveness and faith than it does to build others. You must figure in the assaults and accusations the Enemy will use to attempt to sideswipe you.

Some of the traumatic triggers you'll experience may bring to the surface such great pain that it takes a while to reveal the real root of the division and how it grew between the two of you. Again we must emphasize that forgiveness and faith will result in the construction of a strong bridge than can hold the weight of *any* burden and help you cross over into new territories in your marriage. We will use an example from our own relationship to illustrate this principle.

Near the end of one of our mission trips we experienced a small problem that led to a great divide. It's rather comical to look back on it now and realize that it all started during our time at the Grand Canyon.

Short on time, we'd slipped into a gift shop to pick up a few postcards to send to our supporters and some t-shirts for our families. Somehow in the shuffle, we lost a credit card. Of course, it took several hours for us to realize the credit card was missing, and that's when everything seemed go downhill. Being exhausted didn't help matters. To shorten a long story, losing the credit card seemed to set off one trigger after another and eventually, our conversation came to a halt. There seemed to be a Grand Canyon-sized gap in communication between us. Because we have a standard in our marriage about not raising our voices or speaking rudely to each other, we stopped our discussion and tabled it for a later time.

Believe it or not, it took us several weeks to sort through what transpired and figure out why the experience had instigated such a stalemate. In the meantime, however, we individually went before God to help us forgive what we still didn't understand. Remember, *all* our sins were pardoned when Jesus suffered and died on the cross. Romans 5:8 says, *"But God demonstrates his own love for us in this:* **While** *we were* **yet** *sinners, Christ died for us"* (emphasis added).

Gaining clarity regarding our conflict came slowly—through spending time in God's Word and prayer—but it came. Forgiving each other *before* we were able to come to a resolution and understanding of what happened helped ensure that progress was still being made on building the bridge over this divide. During this time, we still talked to each other and demonstrated love and devotion. We just weren't ready to talk about what had happened.

The faith God required at that time was to fully entrust our frustration, anger, and other feelings into His hands each day while we sorted through the clutter. When we were both ready to talk about what had happened and bring it all to a resolution, we were *continuing* on in the bridge construction process. Progress on our bridge had not been halted due to harboring ill will or unforgiveness.

Our shortcomings and sins can run deep...even spanning several generations. When you find yourselves standing at a chasm of Grand Canyon proportions, chances are you're dealing with much more than just the matter at hand. When we brought the circumstance before God, He revealed the way it was rooted

128

in old strongholds inherited from past generations. Clint's panic over the possibility of identity theft and fraudulent charges stirred up the financial fears he'd lived with for decades. My flippant and carefree attitude about the lost credit card was not at all in tune with what Clint was experiencing. As soon as he shared his feelings with me, I could understand why he reacted the way that he did. He explained that his grandmother had lost everything several times over during the Great Depression and the world wars through which she'd lived. Clint's mother had also endured financial hardship after his father died and Clint had suffered financial problems prior to our remarriage.

Although I couldn't relate to any of those experiences, I now understood where Clint was coming from. In addition, he realized that I wasn't trying to act like what had happened was no big deal when I had suggested that he just lighten up while I made a quick phone call to cancel the card.

Accurately assessing and sifting through a conflict—no matter how painful or involved the process might be—ensures that the bridge you build through forgiveness and faith will do its job. When you intentionally and reverently allow God to work through the pain from your past and mend the gaps in your marriage, He will safely carry you to the other side. Soon, you'll discover that traumatic triggers happen less frequently, and when they do, you'll know exactly how to build over them. In addition, you'll find that God is using these things to enrich your marriage and deepen your dialogue—the topic of our next chapter.

CHAPTER EXERCISES

Prayer to Build Bridges of Forgiveness and Faith

Father, we invite You to examine our hearts and minds. We confess the sins of our past to You, repent of them, and receive Your forgiveness. Help us forgive ourselves and each other. We come to You humbly and ask You to show us the ways You want to change us. Grant us the desire and courage to forgive one another for the ways we've been hurt by each other's actions and words. We ask for Your wisdom to help us deal with the memories that trigger old wounds. When painful memories come, help us recognize them and renounce the Enemy's attempt to divide us. If our circumstances generate responses and emotions based on past generations or our upbringings, clearly reveal these mysteries to us. When memories and pain are triggered, use Your Holy Spirit to remind us of *exactly* what we need to do to honor You and our marriage. Show us the way to build bridges of forgiveness and faith over these painful places. Redeem the poor choices we've made in the past and use them for Your glory. In Jesus' name. Amen.

Identifying Related Issues

Harboring unforgiveness in a relationship is often the source of other issues in your life. Look at the list on the next page and place a check mark next to any of the symptoms you've experienced in the last six months. Is unforgiveness manifesting itself in any of the conditions listed? If so, ask God for the wisdom to deal with these things appropriately. Take some time during the coming week to write down the ways in which these related issues have surfaced. Be willing to seek professional help, if necessary. Many times when the cause is treated, the symptoms cease.

___Depression   ___Anxiety/fear
___Rage   ___Anger
___Physical abuse   ___Chaos
___Obsessive thoughts ___Guilt
___Weight gain/loss   ___Obsessive behaviors
___Sleeplessness   ___Chemical abuse

Scripture Reading

Re-read Nehemiah 2 before answering the questions.

Questions to Consider

1. Do you find it more difficult to extend forgiveness or ask your spouse for forgiveness? Why do you think this is so?

2. Describe a time when you asked someone for forgiveness. What was the person's response and how did it impact you?

3. Is there anyone from whom you need to ask forgiveness? What is holding you back from doing so?

4. What kinds of conversations are the most difficult for you to engage in with your spouse? Why do you think this is so?

5. What do you think the risks were regarding Nehemiah's conversation with King Artaxerxes in Nehemiah 2?

6. Look over the negative events you've listed on your marriage timeline. Are there any areas where you may still be harboring bitterness against your spouse for what occurred? If so, confess those things to God and your spouse. Seek forgiveness. Extend forgiveness.

Very early on in their marriage, Rich and Sharon struggled with communication and conflict resolution. Their conversations stayed at a surface level and revolved around church responsibilities, raising their kids, and life on the farm. They argued constantly. A lack of emotional intimacy eventually took its toll. After seventeen years of marriage and four different counselors, Sharon decided their relationship was hopeless. They separated for a total of sixteen months before things began to change and they figured out how to talk with and listen to each other.

"I wanted to obey God more than I wanted my own way," recalls Sharon. "God taught me that without a doubt, He is trustworthy. He will never leave me and will always walk right beside me through everything—especially the hard times. Most of all, He taught me that when I give Him room to work, He will work miracles."

Besides deepening their individual relationships with God during their separation, Rich and Sharon told us that learning some basic communication tools[7] also helped deepen their dialogue. "Using these skills gave us a safe environment to share our deepest selves—those parts of us that we'd never been able to share with each other. It gave us a way to walk through the past hurts and resolve our conflicts over them."

Continued on the next page…

Continued from the previous page...

Rich and Sharon now teach these same communication tools to other couples. "These tools were the catalyst for the miracle God did in rescuing our marriage. In addition, we used the skills we learned with our kids as well. Now, they are also able to testify to God's faithfulness in their own lives during our marriage and separation."

"Even now, when problems arise, we still pull out those same communication tools and use them," said Rich. "Sharon and I are both sensitive to realize that when we feel ourselves heading for trouble, we will stop our conversation and say, 'We don't want to go there. We better use our tools.'"

Richard and Sharon Wildman
Certified Life/Marriage Coaches
Stubborn Pursuits Ministries
South Charleston, OH

Chapter 7 – Deepening Your Discussions

One of the difficulties you'll encounter during the restoration process is the challenge of re-establishing healthy communication, or perhaps establishing it for the first time. In our case, there was a huge gap between the last time we had spoken to each other (the day our divorce papers were notarized) and our next conversation, more than a decade later. In addition to the time that had elapsed, our last few conversations as husband and wife were strained and far from healthy. However, because we'd both spent years focusing on our individual relationships with God before remarrying, we knew we could rely on Him to help guide us in re-establishing healthy communication.

Like us, it will take time for you to re-establish edifying lines of communication. Again, we can't stress enough that the key to healthy communication is maintaining a reconciled relationship with God and learning to rely on His Holy Spirit for help. Conversations with your spouse (which include speaking *and* listening) should always flow out of your conversations with God. If you're spending time with Him, then communicating with your spouse, no matter how difficult it may be, will gain a more natural rhythm and momentum. You will engage in discussions that are pleasing to God and edifying to each other. Over time, the content of your dialogue will deepen as well.

We refer to the more challenging level of dialogue necessary for the complete restoration of a marriage as *courageous conversation*—a concept we now teach couples in our seminars. The challenge courageous conversation poses for couples who've been through a crisis is that most possess a natural tendency to avoid these kinds of discussions, fearing that they may lead to more conflict. But, we've discovered the opposite. Intentionally engaging in courageous conversation actually alleviates conflict down the road because there is already an underlying understanding between spouses. Moreover, proactively engaging in courageous conversation means that neither spouse is left to flounder in reactive emotions when faced with tense or sticky situations.

The concept we want to get across here is that in order to deepen your dialogue, there will be conversations in your marriage that *feel* risky. They *feel* risky because they *are* risky. However, these conversations are extremely necessary for the overall health and growth of your relationship, as well as its restoration.

We were first introduced to the need for courageous conversation by our trusted mentors. Dale and Colleen shepherded us during the first few years of our remarriage. The honesty and forthrightness in their marriage inspired us to desire more authentic communication in ours. It all began with a question they asked shortly before we were remarried.

"Clint and Penny, how is your marriage affair-proof?" In other words, they wanted to know what plans we'd discussed and made together to eliminate any possibility of placing ourselves (or being placed in) compromising situations. This was dialogue at a whole different level for us.

Over the years since then, we've carefully listened as Dale and Colleen have shared more than thirty years of their courageous conversations, such as their affair-proof marriage plan. To protect their relationship and Dale's position as a pastor, early on in their marriage they talked about and agreed upon certain non-negotiable standards when it came to interacting with others. In other words, they were not afraid to talk openly about staying out of questionable circumstances that might put either of them into a compromising situation with a person of the opposite sex. They even spoke about these agreements with their close friends, like us, to proactively alleviate any misunderstandings down the road. We've been deeply impacted by the ways Dale and Colleen are not afraid to talk about *every* aspect of their marriage so that it consistently pleases God.

Jesus Tackled the Tough Topics

Courageous conversation between most spouses does feel strange, at first. This is exactly why it's deemed *courageous*. The Bible is full of these types of conversations and there was no one who engaged in dicey dialogue with more love, gentleness, and purpose than Jesus. Take, for example, His conversation with the woman at the well in John 4.

> *The woman said to him, "Sir, give me this water so that I won't get thirsty and have to keep coming here to draw water." He told her, "Go, call your husband and come back." "I have no husband," she replied. Jesus said to her, "You are right when you say you have no husband. The fact is, you have had five husbands, and the man you now have is not your husband. What you have just said is quite true."*
>
> John 4:15–18

Jesus' conversation with this woman was courageous in several ways. First, He was taking a double-sized risk by talking to a Samaritan, and a Samaritan *woman* at that. Jews and Samaritans did not associate with one another and it was against social practices for a man and woman to converse alone.

Secondly, Jesus tackled a very tough subject at the well that day. He knew this woman wasn't living in a right relationship with God and that the man she was living with wasn't her husband. Notice, however, that even though Jesus got to the heart of the matter, He did it with love, respect, and compassion. Jesus' willingness to engage in this exchange of dialogue dramatically impacted the woman's life and, for that matter, altered the entire course of human history. Following her conversation with Jesus, the Bible indicates that she went into town and told others about Him (John 4:28–29). As a result of her testimony, many Samaritans believed that Jesus was the Savior of the world (John 4:39–42).

We had no affair-proof plan back when Dale and Colleen asked us that pivotal question, but we have one now. And, it took several courageous conversations for us to get there. Since then, we've had many others. Courageous conversation is now a regular and integral part of our marriage.

Our man, Nehemiah, came face-to-face with a need to effectively and courageously communicate with people from all walks of life. As a layman, we can assume that he wasn't highly-trained in communication skills, especially in regard to dealing with royalty. However, God had divinely gifted this prophet and placed him in positions where quality communication skills were of the utmost importance.

Nehemiah's conversation with King Artaxerxes regarding his desire to leave his position of royal service and return to Jerusalem was definitely on the cutting edge in terms of risk. We can learn a great deal by carefully dissecting his conversation with the king, extracting the essence of his approach and skills, and applying those to marriage. Elements of their conversation as recorded in Nehemiah 2 merit some serious investigation, for they hold the power to transform conversation with your spouse from idle chit-chat and petty arguments into meaningful discussions that will deepen the intimacy in your marriage.

> *In the month of Nisan in the twentieth year of King Artaxerxes, when wine was brought for him, I took the wine and gave it to the king. I had not been sad in his presence before; so the king asked me, "Why does your face look so sad when you are not ill? This can be nothing but sadness of heart." I was very much afraid, but I said to the king, "May the king live forever! Why should my face not look sad when the city where my fathers are buried lies in ruins, and its gates have been destroyed by fire?" The king said to me, "What is it you want?"*
>
> Nehemiah 2:1–4

As the king's cupbearer, Nehemiah had a hazardous job. It was his responsibility to taste everything before it was given to the king. For example, if the king wanted a cup of wine, Nehemiah would drink it first and if he suffered no sickness or death, the king would partake. Even though Nehemiah's job was dangerous, the day he engaged in conversation with the king regarding his desire to return to Jerusalem, his job got a whole lot more risky. He literally put his life on the line because the king had the power to order Nehemiah's execution with the slight movement of his hand.

We must stop here and note that the primary element to consider regarding deeper discussions in your marriage is that there is risk involved. Nehemiah's conversation with the king was extremely courageous. Again, the king had the power to imprison Nehemiah or end his life. Obviously neither of you possesses that kind of power. However, much of the heartache in a broken marriage comes from the words you've said...or should have said, but didn't.

We encourage you not to take the easy way out by giving in to status-quo conversations. Regularly engaging in courageous conversation means that you never give the Enemy an opportunity to derail your marriage through misunderstanding. As the years have passed and our marriage has matured, we've continued to dive into dialogue at a more intimate level than we did when we were married the first time. Let's continue to dissect the additional parts of Nehemiah's conversation in order to discover the six key communication tools that are an integral part of cultivating rich dialogue in your marriage.

Communication Tool 1: Make an Effort to Study Your Spouse

As cupbearer, Nehemiah was often in the king's presence because, as stated earlier, *nothing* passed through the king's lips if it didn't pass over his first. Frequently being in the king's presence meant that Nehemiah knew his likes and dislikes. He observed the ways the king operated and he knew what made him tick. Nehemiah got to know the king and we can safely ascertain that, albeit to a different degree, the king knew Nehemiah as well. They must have had a fairly established relationship otherwise the king never would have noticed the uncharacteristic look of sadness on Nehemiah's face. *"Why does your face look so sad when you are not ill? This can be nothing but sadness of heart"* (Nehemiah 2:2).

There are several additional things you should notice in this passage. You must have an established and sound relationship with God as your King. Like Nehemiah, be in the King's presence often. We may sound like a broken record, but through His Word, prayer, and worship, you must continue to learn God's likes and dislikes as well as to carefully observe the manner in which He works. Make an effort to study God.

The same holds true for your relationship with your mate. Spend time observing him/her, getting to know his/her likes and dislikes, and establishing a relationship of mutual trust. Effective communication grows out of studying and knowing each other. Safety in being vulnerable comes when you spend time together and intentionally work to rebuild trust. (More information on rebuilding trust will be discussed in Chapter 8).

When we remarried, we were overwhelmed by the number of years and events we'd missed in each other's lives and the lives of our families. We felt like we really didn't know each other. Weddings, graduations, birthdays and many other important life experiences had passed during our years apart. In order to help us get to know each other again, we spent time looking through photos and watching videos from our years apart. We also shared journal entries and mementos from special events. The time we spent sharing those things helped us fill in some important missing pieces.

Whether your marriage crisis included separation or not, consider new ways you can deliberately spend time getting to know each other better. There are few things more comforting than being truly known by your spouse and investing your time and energy into increasing your knowledge of him/her. If you were separated and/or divorced, think about ways to communicate the changes that occurred in your life during your time apart. However, be sensitive to your spouse's feelings, reactions, and body language because traumatic triggers can unexpectedly surface when discussing events from the past. Remember, the intent is getting to know each other better and expressing your love, not rehashing old problems.

Communication Tool 2: Honestly Acknowledge Your Feelings of Fear and Discomfort

The king's royal servants were expected to maintain composure at all times. However, Nehemiah candidly confesses he was "very much afraid" before answering the king's question (Nehemiah 2:2). Nehemiah may have been sad and fearful, but he didn't allow fear to paralyze him. Instead, he used his fear to mobilize him toward taking a new step of faith; answering the king's question with confidence and honesty.

Most of the fear you'll face regarding courageous conversation is based on factors such as your past relationships, upbringing, fear of rejection, and the nature of the subject matter being discussed. To illustrate our point, let us introduce you to a couple Clint and I met several years ago.

A couple we'll refer to as Paul and Diane had been married a few years when we first met them. By all outward appearances, they seemed to be progressing along in their relationship. A short time later, however, they hit a point of crisis and came to us for help. Communication was at a standstill. When I had the opportunity to speak with Diane alone, she expressed her fears and struggles in discussing difficult subjects with her husband because of what happened to her as a child. Her primary caretaker, a very dominant and larger-than-life figure, was never approachable and always angry. This person was given to outbursts of anger and Diane was now transferring her childhood experiences of fear and rejection onto her husband, expecting him to respond to her the same way that her caretaker had. As a result, Diane avoided any measure of deep conversation with Paul and stayed at arm's length from him. Diane's upbringing automatically put her at a considerable distance from her husband.

As we walked alongside this couple, we modeled a few basic skills that they were able to adapt to fit their relationship. Paul soon realized that he could help Diane overcome her fears if he would intentionally set aside time to talk, make eye contact, and take an interest in what she was saying. With practice, Paul's gentle demeanor comforted Diane and gave her the courage to speak up and share her feelings with more confidence. While there were other issues to work through, most of them stemmed from not being able to express feelings without a fear of rejection. Since that time, Paul and Diane have steadily put the skills they've learned into practice and both report that they're much closer.

Communication Tool 3: Demonstrate Affirmation and Admiration

Nehemiah wasn't buttering up his boss when he exclaimed, *"May the king live forever!"* (Nehemiah 2:3). This was a common form of address to communicate respect to a king.

How do you commonly address your spouse? With respect? With love? Sometimes a word of affirmation, an appreciative tone of voice, or intentionally communicating kindness will make all the difference. If your mate thinks that every discussion is going to be miserable or that he/she is going to be disrespected, devalued, or belittled, he/she will be reluctant to talk openly or listen.

As far as I (Clint) am concerned, praising and affirming each other as we tackle the tough topics has made a lot of difference in healing my reluctance to discuss my feelings and opinions. When we were married the first time, I shut down during difficult conversations because I felt like my opinions and feelings were going to be judged. I now understand that this stemmed from experiences in my past. Unfortunately, before I met Penny I had a history of relationships that left me wounded when I reached out and risked vulnerability. Eventually, I gave up on sharing my thoughts, feelings, or opinions. By the time Penny and I were married, I'd made a subconscious decision to remain closed to conversations that required me to be vulnerable.

When we remarried, I told Penny about my struggles and expressed my desire to change. Just admitting a reluctance to share my true feelings and emotions helped Penny realize she could encourage me by being a good listener. Since then, she's affirmed me when I have new ideas or when I tell her my hopes and fears. In addition, during our discussions, Penny makes a point of complimenting the changes she sees in me regarding my openness and vulnerability. Her demeanor and kindness have made me want to share more and more of my heart with her.

Communication Tool 4: Bathe Courageous Conversation in Prayer

Before Nehemiah told the king what was troubling him, he prayed. *"Then I prayed to the God of heaven, and I answered the king"* (Nehemiah 2:4). Nehemiah's prayer isn't explained in any detail so we don't know exactly what he said to God in those moments. But, we can assume it was probably something like, "Oh Lord, I'm nervous! Help me say what *You* want me to say!"

It's important that whenever you're going to engage in a courageous conversation, you first spend time praying about it on your own. I think of Jesus as my first husband and Clint as

144

my second. When there's something important I need to discuss with Clint, I take it to Jesus first. Sometimes, I only get as far as bringing the matter before Him and He lets me know that it's not the right time to bring it up to Clint or that I need to make a change in my heart regarding the concern.

Praying before a courageous conversation will help you share ideas and concerns with added love and gentleness. Prayer also makes you a more humble listener.

In addition to prayer, Clint and I never enter into these discussions without stating up-front that we'll be treading on holy ground. It's our way of giving each other a heads-up. You may find it helpful to give your spouse some advance notice when the need for a courageous conversation arises. That way, your mate has time to prepare his/her heart and together, you can choose an opportune time to talk. As a rule, courageous conversations should always be bathed in prayer before and after, and should be held in the privacy of your own home or a quiet place that is free from distractions.

Communication Tool 5: Humbly Ask for What You Need

Nehemiah was specific with the king, letting him know exactly what he needed to be successful regarding his journey to Jerusalem.

> *The king said to me, "What is it you want?" Then I prayed to the God of heaven, and I answered the king, "If it pleases the king and if your servant has found favor in his sight, let him send me to the city in Judah where my fathers are buried so that I can rebuild it."*
> Nehemiah 2:4–5

I used to find it extremely difficult to communicate my needs to Clint. I'd much rather have had him read my mind and instinctively know what I needed, without my having to tell him. That kind of thinking created huge problems in our first marriage and it's been a challenge for us this time around as well. Based on some experiences in my past, I'm reluctant to say what I need or want. Instead, I allow my needs to dance around in my head, sometimes for weeks or months.

Over time, I finally learned to use the same principle discussed earlier about bringing my needs before Jesus as my first husband and Clint as my second. In prayer, I tell the Lord what I need because I know He is more than capable of meeting all my needs. Then, I let the Holy Spirit decide if my needs should be communicated to Clint and, if so, how I should go about sharing them with him. During the years we've been remarried, I've had many opportunities to practice this process and I learn a little more each time I take a risk to do so.

Based on Nehemiah's conversation with the king, there are two other important things to note about communicating your needs to your mate. First of all, there are times when you must be direct and concise. Nehemiah wanted to be released from his responsibilities as the king's cupbearer so that he could go to Jerusalem. So, that's exactly what he asked for. Nehemiah was clear about his needs and communicated them with confidence and respect. He wasn't demanding, but he knew how and when to cut right to the chase.

Wives, Nehemiah's tactics here are especially helpful in communicating with your husbands. In general, most men like their wives to spare them from all the details and instead, to get right to point. I've often heard husbands say, "Just give me the bottom line."

I admit that I tend to go for detailed explanations and feel the need to share all the connections I see between the matters at hand. But, I've come to realize that sometimes Clint gets a glossy-eyed look when I've given him too many details. It took me a while to figure this out and to not let it frustrate me. With time and careful observation, I finally realized that Clint and I process information and details at different rates and that our brains are wired in such a way that the *kinds* of details we each want to know about a situation are very different. He likes information involving numbers and patterns and he can remember anything that has to do with measurements, numbers, operations, or visual models. On the other hand, I like details regarding feelings and remember experiential things that are tied to emotion and beauty. We finally realized that these differences must be taken into account when we communicate with one another.

Like most couples, we fall into the general stereotype that women tend to use more words and other means of communication (such as, gestures, body language, facial expressions, etc.) than men. Clint says it jokingly, but accurately in our seminars. "My wife needs to use about 20,000 words a day. I've learned that I have to let her get those words out. I only need to use about 10,000. But, I love my wife so much that I give her 5,000 of my words so she can really have a good time."

Given the drastic differences between the sexes, there must be a give-and-take in communication. It can't be all your way, or your spouse's way. You must both learn to beat the statistics and stereotypes and come to a compromise.

Having said that, there is also a time and place for more details (whether your spouse cares for them, or not). Nehemiah must be commended for breaking male stereotypes. Even though he didn't go into a lot of detail with the king at first, he wasn't afraid to explain things further when he needed to.

> *Then the king, with the queen sitting beside him, asked me, "How long will your journey take, and when will you get back?" It pleased the king to send me; so I set a time. I also said to him, "If it pleases the king, may I have letters to the governors of Trans-Euphrates, so that they will provide me safe-conduct until I arrive in Judah? And may I have a letter to Asaph, keeper of the king's forest, so he will give me timber to make beams for the gates of the citadel by the temple and for the city wall and for the residence I will occupy?"*
>
> Nehemiah 2:6–8

One commentary suggests Nehemiah and the queen probably carried on many side conversations while the king was busy conducting the affairs of his kingdom. Perhaps the queen rubbed off on Nehemiah a bit. Whatever the case, he seemed to strike the perfect balance between not saying enough and saying too much. We can all stand to learn from his lead.

Communication Tool 6: Courageous Conversation Should Please the King

Nehemiah uses the phrase, *"If it pleases the king,"* twice in Nehemiah 2 (verses 5 and 7). He wanted to be sure all his requests were in alignment with what would honor the king. Our conversations should also have, as their goal, God's pleasure and honor, not just ours. When the desire of your heart is to please God, harsh tones, negative statements, and outbursts of anger will be eliminated. That doesn't mean your dialogue will be dull or void of emotion, by any means. Nehemiah displayed emotion when he was sad of heart in the king's presence. Remember, he was so visibly upset that the king took notice of his emotional state (Nehemiah 2:1–2).

Sometimes emotions get a bad rap, but deep discussions should include the appropriate expression of your emotions. *Appropriate* is the key word here. God has emotions and He carefully wired us with them as well. The Holy Spirit can temper emotions that aren't pleasing to God, such as outbursts of anger or rage.

I (Penny) grew up having quite a temper. To put it plainly, I said my first cuss word at the age of four. By the time I was ten, I had increased my gruff vocabulary and learned how to punch my way through elementary school. It took a lot of hard work, but once I finally brought my anger before God, the Holy Spirit began to sand off my rough edges. When people come to us and admit a problem with anger, I can tell them with great confidence that if they really want to make a change, God will show them just how to do it!

In order to help you engage in discussions that are pleasing to God, we've developed a list of ground rules that will require a commitment on the part of both spouses. You will also find it helpful to review these commitments periodically.

Our Courageous Conversation Commitments

- We will pray before/after our courageous conversations.
- We will reveal our disappointments and inner fears.
- We will not reject each other.
- We will keep our hearts open and vulnerable.
- We will listen and not interrupt.

Continued on the next page…

Our Courageous Conversation Commitments

- We will make it safe to be honest with one another.
- We will not use anything said to one another as ammunition down the road.
- We will not attempt to manipulate, intimidate, or control each other.
- We will consider things from each other's viewpoint.
- We will not use harsh/rude tones or foul language.
- We will not place blame, make accusations, engage in fault finding, or throw things from the past in each other's faces.
- We will hold each other accountable to God's desired outcomes.
- We will seek God's will each day by spending time alone with Him.
- We will not force each other to meet needs or expectations.
- We will reach out to one another with affection and prayer.
- We will not withdraw emotionally or physically during conversation.
- We will apologize, seek forgiveness, and extend forgiveness to each other.
- We will view conflict as an opportunity for growth.

It's so tempting to sweep sensitive issues under the carpet because they're awkward to discuss. Remember, though, whatever is kept in the dark can roadblock your relationship when you least expect it. Courageous conversations may be uncomfortable, but God can use these experiences for His good purposes. Like Nehemiah, you'll discover that when you prayerfully and intentionally engage in courageous conversations, the final outcome is well worth the risk.

And because the gracious hand of my God was upon me, the king granted my requests. So I went to the governors of Trans-Euphrates and gave them the king's letters. The king had also sent army officers and cavalry with me.

Nehemiah 2:8–9

CHAPTER EXERCISES

Prayer to Deepen Your Discussions

Father, we want our conversations to please You and to be meaningful to our marriage. We need Your help. Please reveal the areas in which we need to communicate with more compassion, kindness, and honesty. Help us speak with humility, the way You did. Jesus, You never failed to communicate love and understanding, or to listen as people asked You questions and expressed their feelings. Show us how to learn these skills. Use Your Holy Spirit to keep us in check when we fail to communicate in a healthy way and to temper our emotions. Help us get to know one another better so we can learn how to effectively communicate, especially when it comes to handling tough topics. We understand there is a risk involved in deepening our discussions. We are willing to take that risk, but we can't do it without You. Grant us a more intimate relationship through meaningful conversation. In Jesus' name we pray. Amen.

Making Connections

Write down some possible topics for courageous conversations that you think should occur in your marriage at this time, or in the future. Commit to praying about these conversations, as well as God's timing for engaging in them. Ask Him for wisdom before moving forward, but don't put off what you know must take place.

Questions to Consider

1. Describe the ways in which each of the following things contributes to courageous conversation: prayer, trust, honesty, body language, and cultural background.

2. Discuss some of your thoughts/concerns about having courageous conversations. Can you think of any relationship or situation that caused conflict which could have been reduced or alleviated had a courageous conversation taken place beforehand?

3. Technological advances (such as the Internet, e-mail, explicit movie channels, etc.) have created easy opportunities for people to get themselves into compromising situations. How might a courageous conversation be helpful?

4. Discuss how you would be feeling right now if you were in Nehemiah's shoes at this point in the rebuilding project (impatient, hopeful, focused, fearful, determined, frustrated, etc.). Are there ways in which these feelings mirror your outlook on the restoration of your marriage? Be honest.

5. Have you been adding positive and negative events to your marriage timeline? If not, take some time to do so and discuss the ways proactive conversation can help to positively impact rough situations. Also, be sure to note times where there was a difference in the way you and your spouse viewed the same life event, i.e., one of you viewed the event as positive and the other person viewed that same event as negative. Did your difference of opinion cause problems between you?

Rebuilding trust and intimacy has been a daily process, ever since we reconciled in 1991. We both realize there are some deep wounds the Enemy can raise up at any moment and we do not ever take our reconciliation for granted. When old triggers from past pain or conflict creep into our relationship, we wait for the panicky thoughts to subside. Then, we both put truth into the situation.

One thing that triggers old stuff for me (Michelle) is when I take longer to get home than I expected and Joe calls to ask me what's taking so long. I have to be really careful that I don't assume he is mistrusting me, but simply wants to know when I'll be home.

For me (Joe) an old button gets pushed when I start to feel left out of the loop in planning. I have to remind myself that it's my responsibility to speak up and ask Michelle to update my calendar, rather than assume she is leaving me out of something because she doesn't want me there.

Joe and Michelle Williams
Founders of the *International Center for Reconciling God's Way* and Authors of *Yes, Your Marriage Can Be Saved*
Modesto, CA

Chapter 8 – Rebuilding on the Ruins of Your Past

A resilient relationship that can weather life's storms requires a deep level of mutual trust between spouses. Building mutual trust in a marriage isn't something that just happens naturally and rebuilding trust after a crisis, separation, or divorce poses added challenges. It's a process that must be deliberately cultivated and nurtured. Most of all, rebuilding trust requires prayer, practice, courageous conversation, and a willingness to work together, especially regarding the specific places where trust was betrayed.

As a marriage grows, there are levels of trust through which the relationship should progress. Because every marriage is unique, there is no rule book about what you discover at each level, how you get there, or exactly when trust will take root. One thing can be said of all marriages, however. As you learn to trust God, He teaches you how to trust each another. This chapter specifically focuses on the ways you can rebuild trust in your marriage or, depending upon your history together, begin building a foundation of trust for the first time.

During our first marriage we were stuck in a shallow level of trust and never progressed beyond that level. Why? Because we didn't know how to nurture trust in our relationship. We didn't realize it would take time and a diligent effort to develop mutual trust, and that as we intentionally practiced trusting God and each other, our trust would grow. The lack of trust in our first marriage was also due, in part, to the fact that we were unwilling to risk being completely honest with each other. Neither one of us wanted to come off as weak, wimpy, or needy, so we maintained a stiff upper lip no matter how tough things got. Translation: we were too proud to be vulnerable. A pattern of toughing it out was repeated over and over again in both of our lives.

To complicate matters, we'd both experienced other relationships where trust was severely shattered and intimacy was violated. As a result, we subconsciously made an agreement never to let anyone get too close. During the two years we dated, we were mutually attracted to what we perceived was a tremendous amount of strength and self-discipline in each other's personalities. What we didn't realize was that underneath our respective façades was raw pain that, for most of our lives, had been unaddressed and layered over with a veneer of self-protection and pride. When we hit our first major conflict, all our unaddressed hurts rose up and broke through the surface. Instead of getting some help to deal with these hurts and losses, the pain overflowed into every aspect of our relationship and obscured our understanding of what was really going on.

During the years we were divorced, we both received some biblically-based counseling. Devoting the time it takes to heal and seeking God for our individual restoration was worth every penny spent. Neither of us realized how much hurt and loss we'd stuffed down and sucked up as a result of the severed trust in our lives, or how those experiences contributed to the ways we interacted as husband and wife. Unfortunately, the intimacy that marriage requires is often the perfect catalyst for unaddressed pain to surface. Like many couples, instead of honestly disclosing our wounds to each other, we covered them over and kept on going. But, you can only live like that for so long. Eventually, something's got to give or the marriage is going to give way.

It's highly likely that your crisis, separation, and/or divorce also involved broken trust and losses that were never grieved. Before we proceed with the remainder of this chapter, we want to give you a necessary word of caution. While we share some of our experiences and those of others in order to help you learn how to rebuild trust, remember that the specific ways God restored trust in these marriages may differ from how He restores trust in yours. In other words, the stories we share are not meant to be prescriptive. They won't serve to spoon-feed you with a step-by-step list or logical order as to exactly what you should do to deepen trust. Every marriage survival story is different. But, we share these stories with you because we believe they're extremely valuable to your journey and we're confident there are generalizations within them that will apply to your circumstances. Suspend making decisions as to how you'll approach rebuilding trust in your relationship until you've read the entire chapter and prayed fervently. It matters that much.

Hitting Rock Bottom

Shortly after remarrying, we had the opportunity to visit Israel with a group from our church. Touring Jerusalem and taking in the sites was fascinating, but it was the time spent walking amongst the ruins of Beth Shean that impacted our marriage beyond anything we'd expected. Located on the ancient trade routes between Mesopotamia and the Mediterranean Sea, Beth Shean was a large city that eventually fell to the Philistines in the 11th century BC (1 Samuel 31). Centuries later, Beth Shean became a flourishing city under the Byzantines until economic collapse and an earthquake in AD 749 reduced it to rubble.

"That's what our marriage looked like when we hit bottom," Clint whispered as we walked together, snapping photos at every turn. He was right. When our marriage came crashing down, it was nothing more than scattered rubble and debris. Any shallow measure of trust that we had developed during our brief marriage was completely shattered when we separated and divorced.

While in Israel, our guide explained that archaeologists have been excavating the ruins at Beth Shean over a period of many years. During our tour, we were fortunate to see some of the partial reconstruction of its ancient streets, columns, and walls. As a result of that experience, we realized the powerful analogy between the work of the archaeologists to rebuild the ancient city and the trust we needed to build into our marriage. For the purposes of this chapter, we'll use this analogy to further describe the ways you and your spouse—like trained archaeologists—can learn from your past in order to rebuild for your future. Consider what we offer here as a new suite of tools to add to your marriage tool belt.

Rediscovering the Past

The day we walked around Beth Shean, we were quite impressed by the oddly-shaped hills surrounding the site: hills with steep inclines and perfectly flat tops. Our tour guide explained that these particular hills were commonly referred to as *tels* (as in *Tel Aviv.*) A tel is formed when ruined civilizations are leveled and new civilizations are built on top of the same site. Over time, the level of each new city rises, hence the tel's distinct shape. As a result of the ongoing excavation at Beth Shean, civilizations dating from the Early Bronze Age to the Medieval Period had been discovered at that one site, with each new civilization building on the successive one. Our guide went on to explain that, for a variety of political, economic, and religious reasons, rebuilding a new civilization on top of a ruined one was a common practice for thousands of years.

We see evidence of this practice in the Bible. The book of Jeremiah records the following account regarding the future restoration of Israel following their captivity:

> *"But I will restore you to health and heal your wounds," declares the LORD, "because you are called an outcast, Zion for whom no one cares." This is what the LORD says: "I will restore the fortunes of Jacob's tents and have compassion on his dwellings; the city will be rebuilt **on her ruins**, and the palace will stand in its proper place."*
>
> Jeremiah 30:17–18 (emphasis added)

Retired archaeologist, K. Kris Hurst, speculates that civilizations built on the ruins of predecessors to obtain a clear conscience.[8] In other words, her research indicates that civilizations built on past ruins to wipe the slate clean and start over. Their desire was to do it better than it had been done before.

The same can be said for the ruins in your relationship. Some of your marriage ruins exist because trust was broken along the way, but the slate can be cleared and you can start over. Getting a fresh start begins when you acknowledge the painful experiences that have occurred in your marriage and ask God to rebuild your relationship in those very same areas. Although it isn't easy to revisit the past, God can be trusted with the process. He will never malign your trust or take advantage of you. God is incapable of breaking trust because He is holy and perfect. Acknowledge that God is the only One capable of perfect trust and ask Him to show you how to nurture and build trust in the exact places where trust was broken.

For example, because our marriage history included infidelity, we had a lot of work to do in that specific area. Today, there are some outstanding resources available to help couples rebuild trust after infidelity but, back then, we felt unsure about exactly how to proceed and didn't realize others had successfully navigated these waters before us. Even though our lack of knowledge and resources posed a challenge, the benefit was that we learned to consistently go before God and ask Him for help.

One of our most intimate experiences in the process of rebuilding trust took place when Penny shared something with me that she'd written many years before our lives intersected again. One of the assignments she completed during her time in counseling was to write down her sexual history. What Penny wrote included some painful events from her childhood and adolescence, as well as some experiences later in her life. Of course, she never imagined she'd ever be sharing these intimate secrets with me, of all people.

Before reading her sexual history to me, Penny explained that she needed to return to these painful places where intimacy and trust were broken in order to truly heal. While she took full responsibility for her choices at the end of our first marriage, she'd also learned how other inappropriate sexual incidents had banded together and risen to the surface, giving her the added fuel to walk out and never look back. In her eyes, I was just another guy who had let her down.

Like an archaeologist, Penny was carefully exposing the past in order to learn from it and change her future. I'll never forget how I felt as she read what she'd written.

"I'm so sorry. I had no idea," I said, choking back the tears.

Penny's willingness to expose her ruins made me want to share mine. Using my journals from our years apart, I told Penny about the places in my past where intimacy was violated and I revealed the shame I'd unknowingly carried from these traumatic incidents. Disclosing my secrets helped Penny see that what we now refer to as my, "John Wayne suck-it-up personality" had simply been a form of self-protection and self-preservation.

Since then, our times of exposing past secrets to each other have definitely been some of our most intimate moments. These experiences also nurtured and deepened the trust in our relationship. By prayerfully excavating the ruins from our past, we've been able to put more of the pieces together as to why our first marriage didn't make it. This process also allowed God to take those broken pieces and, from them, mold and shape a new marriage that we never dreamed was possible.

Rebuilding Trust with Tenderness

Before an archaeologist begins excavating a site, he/she thoroughly surveys the landscape in order to note the location of specific points of interest. Then he/she gathers important data and decides how to approach the dig. The archaeologist also figures out which tools should be used in each area of the site. Once the excavation begins, the archaeological team proceeds with great care, using fine tools and precise instruments in the most delicate areas. Because the site may contain rare and fragile treasures, trained archaeologists know it's wise to err on the side of caution when digging. In delicate places, a magnifying glass, a small trowel, and a fine brush are used to dust off years of dirt and grit.

The same holds true for the process of exposing the ruins of your past and rebuilding trust in those places. Some of the exercises you've completed in this book (such as making your marriage timeline and the inventory of your roadblocks) are like a survey of your marriage landscape. As you continue the restoration process in these delicate areas, it's essential to proceed with tenderness. Ask the Holy Spirit to help you blow the cakes of dust off the places of past betrayal and expose what needs to be exposed to the healing light of Christ. An important goal of this whole process is to understand what happened in the past and identify the kind of tool that should be used to rebuild trust for each person.

One of the interesting things we learned when conducting research for this book was that there are archaeologists who specialize in recovering evidence from battlefields and war zones in order to have truth rise from the ruins. It would be advantageous for you to consider yourselves *battlefield archaeologists* who want to learn as much as possible from conflicts of the past so that these battles and wars are never repeated. In the areas of your marriage where wounds may still be raw and emotions fragile, demonstrate gentleness and care. Most importantly, when working through tender areas, don't use a backhoe! These places require the use of fine instruments, a skilled hand, and a gentle heart. Again, we will use an example from our own restoration to explain.

Several months after I received Penny's letter of apology and we started seeking God about reconciliation, we decided to meet face-to-face. We felt that spending some quality time together would help us know if it was God's will for us to remarry. Because we wanted our time together to be free from distractions, we decided to meet on neutral territory between my home in Florida, and Penny's home in California. We set a date to meet on Memorial Day weekend in 2002. Before meeting, we both committed to handling our physical contact appropriately; maintaining healthy boundaries and having separate hotel rooms. We also asked a group of mature believers to pray for us and hold us accountable.

After much anticipation, for the first time in over a decade, Penny and I set eyes on each another in the terminal of the Denver International Airport. Our reunion was something we'll never forget. When we share our testimony of reconciliation, we tell people that our first embrace felt like slipping a familiar hand into a tailored glove—a perfect, seamless fit.

By far, one of the most important things we did that weekend was to get honest with each other regarding the specific places in our past where trust had been broken and to expose the guilt and shame we'd carried. This was extremely delicate work, to say the least.

On Saturday morning, we packed a picnic lunch and drove to a park in downtown Denver. There, in a secluded spot, we spread out a blanket and unpacked some of the journals we'd kept during our years apart. For several hours, we took turns reading old entries, talking about the past, and weeping together. Because we never intended to share those journals with anyone but God, the thoughts we'd written down were raw and honest. We asked each other many questions that day and disclosed details from our pasts that we'd never shared with anyone.

During our time in the park, Penny answered all the questions I had about the affair that ended our marriage, as well as many other things that had transpired between us. Penny asked me several poignant questions as well.

At one point in our conversation, I remember looking at Penny and asking, "Didn't you know you were the love of my life?"

"No, Clint...I really didn't."

Penny's response gave me the opportunity to apologize to her for never communicating the depth of my love when we were married, and it helped me understand how she felt back then. Because we'd bathed our time together in prayer and had other people praying for us, our courageous conversations that weekend—as difficult as they may have been—were full of tenderness and compassion.

Since then, we've come to understand that we should never be afraid of engaging in those kinds of discussions, especially regarding intimacy and trust. As stated in the last chapter, these are difficult topics to talk about, but well worth the discomfort.

A powerful way to jump-start this kind of discussion and rebuild trust is by extending the marriage timeline you created together at the end of Chapter 1. Each spouse should use a different colored pen and extend the timeline back into your individual childhoods to identify any places where trust and intimacy were violated or betrayed. Tracing back these specific issues over your life will allow you to naturally engage in the kinds of deep discussions we advocate. This will also help you identify the ways those violations contributed to the crisis in your marriage, as well as providing some explanations (not justifications) for your attitudes and behaviors.

As you discuss the past, it's imperative that you always give your spouse the gift of your discretion. The intimate things disclosed in private shouldn't be discussed with others without having your spouse's permission. In general, it isn't appropriate to share something your spouse has asked you to keep to yourself (unless of course, someone's life is in danger). Use wise judgment. Nothing breaks trust faster than a breech in confidentiality between spouses.

What the Evidence Tells Us

Another part of an archaeologist's job is to accurately interpret the evidence they excavate. He/she carefully studies, catalogues, classifies, and analyzes all the artifacts unearthed during a dig in an effort to discover the answer to one important question: What do these treasures tell us? We didn't realize it at the time, but we now understand that through the process of revisiting our past, we were doing the very same thing. Instead of looking at our history with shame and confusion as we had for decades, we finally viewed what was unearthed as rare treasure (which is exactly how God saw it all along).

That weekend in Denver, we put God in charge of reconstructing the past in order to help us create a more meaningful future. Through this process, we were able to take the ancient relics from our lives, gain a greater understanding about our past behaviors, and figure out why our first marriage failed so miserably in such a short period of time. All the mysteries we'd wondered about for years finally made sense.

Throughout the time we've been on the marriage mission field, we've met other couples who, like us, decided to take an honest look at what really transpired in their marriages in order to learn from the evidence they uncovered. We first met Scott and Cathy after a workshop we were teaching for pastors and ministry leaders. The outright honesty they exhibited in unpacking their saved marriage story with us was proof that they had done the hard work of dusting off all the drama from their crisis and uncovering the real root of their division. After getting to know this couple, we asked them about the excavation process they had gone through and the ways it had positively impacted their marriage.

"It wasn't easy," said Scott. "But I really felt that in order to truly heal our relationship, we both had to be willing to pray through all the deep darkness and bring everything into the light."

Cathy continued their story.

"Opening the lines of communication about our pasts meant we had to be vulnerable with each other. But, as a result, what we have together now exceeds what I ever imagined our marriage could be. People talk about wanting a fairytale marriage. What Scott and I have is far better."

Talking about Trust

As with any grand-scale excavation, rebuilding trust is a process that occurs over a period of months and years. It takes a commitment to intentional, meaningful, and courageous conversation, as well as the development of good listening skills. We found it helpful to regularly schedule uninterrupted times to talk about rebuilding trust in specific areas, especially during our first two years back together. During these conversations, Penny asked me questions such as, "How are you feeling about my friendships with others? Do you have any concerns you'd like to share with me? Is there anything I'm doing that is causing you not to trust me?"

These questions gave me a welcome opportunity to share any concerns or feelings I had regarding my trust in her. During these conversations, we both knew, in advance, that we were entering into intentional discussions about trust, instead of just reacting to an awkward circumstance or catching each other off-guard.

Asking important questions about trust went both ways. I didn't want Penny to live with a shadow of mistrust hanging over her head whenever I wasn't around, and she didn't either. To alleviate this, I would ask her questions such as, "Do you feel like you have the freedom to be with others? Do you sense that I'm trying to control you in any way?" My questions provided Penny with the opportunity to share her feelings and pinpoint her specific concerns about trust. As we regularly engaged in this back-and-forth process, we noticed greater trust forming in our marriage.

Let me take a time-out to speak directly to those of you who may have walked out on your marriage or who may feel the brunt of the blame for what transpired. Even though our first marriage ended when Penny left, I never wanted her to feel like she was "the one" who should bear all the blame for our divorce. I know my closed demeanor and tough-guy attitude also contributed to the breakdown of our marriage. Indicating, through my behavior and words, that Penny should just "suck-it-up" when it came to our problems was definitely not keeping the lines of communication open. My lack of emotion and compassion made it difficult for her to tell me anything. Therefore in our remarriage, I had to work just as hard to rebuild trust with Penny as she did with me. The bottom line is that no matter who did what in your marriage, rebuilding trust is a two-way street.

Regularly setting aside time to talk about trust also means we have learned ways to reaffirm our trust in each other. One of the things we quickly realized was that what I needed Penny to do in order to demonstrate trust was different than what she needed from me. For example, trust was rebuilt for me when Penny would leave a note on the counter when she went somewhere. That way, when I came home to an empty house, I knew why it was empty and where she had gone. Each time Penny left me a note like that, it helped rebuild my trust in her.

During our discussions, I also told Penny I was concerned about getting so busy that we wouldn't have time for each other. This was definitely a problem in our first marriage. At one point, we didn't have much contact other than to hit the pillow and mutter, "Goodnight." Our lack of meaningful interaction made it easier for the gap between us to widen over time. When we remarried, I was concerned that, if we weren't careful, the same thing could happen again. Having us head off in too many different directions was (and still is) a major red flag for me.

While Penny may not have necessarily shared this concern to the same degree, she wanted to demonstrate that she respected my feelings and would work to build trust in this area. Therefore, even to this day, she makes it a priority to keep ample margin and down time in our schedules. There are busy seasons for every family, but for the most part, we've learned how to avoid getting over-committed. Understanding and respecting what I need to rebuild trust helps Penny demonstrate trust in meaningful ways.

For Penny, trust was (and still is) rebuilt in our marriage when she feels the freedom to honestly disclose her greatest fears and worries, without reservation. She isn't accustomed to letting anyone into those vulnerable places. But now, I know that about her. Therefore, I make a point of listening to her concerns with compassion. Because I know she is hesitant to express her feelings and needs, I've learned to ask specific questions such as, "What do you need from me right now? Do you want any help, or do you just want me to listen?"

Like most men, my tendency is to swoop in and solve my wife's problems. Over time I've finally learned that most often, Penny doesn't want me to fix anything. What she wants is for me

168

to listen to her and to know her. Supportive reactions cause Penny to trust me with her feelings to a greater degree. On the other hand, if I withdraw my support or am not interested in her concerns, she feels distant from me and rather than growing, trust between us becomes stagnant.

Our conversations about trust also give us the opportunity to comment on the ways we notice each other intentionally demonstrating meaningful trust. Making a point to acknowledge and compliment each other's efforts will deepen the intimacy in your marriage and draw you closer together.

We encourage you to take some initiative to get to know the specific areas about which your spouse is concerned in regard to trusting you. This will take several courageous conversations. As you engage in these discussions, mark the red flag areas that come up for your spouse and discuss the ways you can respect his/her concerns. Remember, you may not share those same feelings (or understand why these things are important to your mate) but you can ask God to help you come up with ways to demonstrate respect for what your spouse needs.

Rebuilding Trust with Your Children

We've waited until this point in *Marriage on the Mend* to begin talking more specifically about the children (biological and/or step-children) who may be involved in your restoration. As former public school educators, we witnessed the fall-out of troubled marriages on the faces of our students every day. The stress children internalize from what occurs between their parents (and/or step-parents) often manifests itself in the classroom and on the playground. For example, students who are caught in the middle of marital turmoil often have difficulty focusing on their class work and, as a result, their progress in school wanes. Inappropriate behavior, missing homework assignments, and even poor physical health are just a few of the external signs that there may be problems in the home. It's important to realize that your crisis, separation, and/or divorce has dramatically impacted your children's trust in you. You must be willing to rise up, shelter them from further harm, and intentionally rebuild trust in your relationship with each child involved.

Many times, couples get so caught up in their marriage crisis that they pay little attention to the tremendous effect the discord is having on their kids. Security and safety are some of the basic core needs that children possess. Their parents' marriage crisis threatens their sense of security in significant ways. Your children will need a great deal of reassurance as the family is being restored. Children must have a stable environment with set routines and expectations to combat and level out upheaval or chaos they may have experienced in the past.

Marriage problems stir up a great deal of uncertainty that children often absorb in an effort to cope with their surroundings. Some children even feel responsible for the problems between their parents. I (Penny) remember the difficulties my siblings and I encountered when my parents announced their decision to divorce. Somehow, I incorrectly assumed that I was a significant part of the problem. When my parents separated, the three younger children went to live with my mother and the three older children stayed with my father. Our whole world was torn in two and I unwittingly assumed the responsibility for fixing it. Many years later, I realized that each one of us coped (and is still coping) with my parents' divorce in different ways; according to our personalities, perceptions, and ages at the time.

Be intentional about including your children in the process of restoration. Your overall goal is to protect your family unit and to provide for the immediate emotional, physical, and spiritual needs of each child. Take a look at the way Nehemiah recognized the importance of protecting the institution of the family during the restoration of Jerusalem:

Meanwhile, the people in Judah said, "The strength of the laborers is giving out, and there is so much rubble that we cannot rebuild the wall." Also our enemies said, "Before they know it or see us, we will be right there among them and will kill them and put an end to the work." Then the Jews who lived near them came and told us ten times over, "Wherever you turn, they will attack us." Therefore I stationed some of the people behind the lowest points of the wall at the exposed places, posting them by families, with their swords, spears and bows.

Nehemiah 4:10–13

Nehemiah recognized that if a builder was working on a section of the wall that was located far away from his home, he wouldn't be able to protect his family. So, he specifically stationed workers by family groups and armed them with weapons to combat the attacks of their enemies.

It's critical for you to regularly call your children together and arm them with strategies to deal with the struggles they've encountered as a result of your crisis. There are a number of excellent ministries listed in the back of this book that will provide you with resources and help. Don't ever be too proud to seek professional assistance.

Trusting that mom and dad really are going to stay together is a huge hurdle your kids will need help getting over. Because the strength of our entire existence is based upon the family unit, Satan wants nothing more than to tear families apart through betrayal and broken trust. Not only are you in a fight to restore your marriage, but you are in a fight for your family as well.

> *After I looked things over, I stood up and said to the nobles, the officials and the rest of the people, "Don't be afraid of them. Remember the Lord, who is great and awesome, and fight for your brothers, your sons and your daughters, your wives and your homes." When our enemies heard that we were aware of their plot and that God had frustrated it, we all returned to the wall, each to his own work.*
>
> Nehemiah 4:14–15

Part of Nehemiah's strategy for the welfare and protection of the family unit was to help them "remember the Lord." This was Nehemiah's rallying cry in the midst of repeated attacks because he knew that remembering all that God had done would dispel the present fears of the people.

Remembering the Lord should be the rallying cry of your family as well. The most effective way to help your family remember Him is to regularly gather for prayer and intentional conversation about how things are going. Specifically pray with your children to rebuild trust and unity as a family. Consider a weekly family meeting to talk specifically about any concerns that need to be addressed regarding the restoration and healing process. In addition, have your family memorize a Scripture verse each week. Some families find it helpful to keep a journal that serves as a record of their meetings. This journal can also contain prayer requests and answers to prayer which will be an important way of reminding yourselves of all that God has done and is doing.

An unfortunate consequence of marital turmoil is that sometimes children are exposed to much more than they should be. In the midst of heated arguments or attempts to retaliate, spouses often disclose things to their children that should never be revealed. Sometimes young children discover the specific violations that occurred (such as infidelity or addiction) on their own or by overhearing adult conversations. Other times, in anger or retaliation, things have been intentionally disclosed. Whatever the case may be, the trust and security that a child may have had in one or both parents is shaken to the core.

If trust has been violated between you and your children, you'll have some added work to do. That work begins with prayer. Ask God what each child specifically needs in order to rebuild and restore their trust in you. Recognize that, for many children, rebuilding trust takes a great deal of time, depending upon their ages, personalities, the history of your relationship, and the nature of what transpired. If you were separated from your kids, they will feel a sense of abandonment. They may even worry that each time an argument occurs, you'll separate again. In that case, give your kids a safe place to discuss their fears and be certain you address those concerns on a regular basis. Reassure your children that, although their mom and dad will still have differences, you're both committed to making your marriage work and keeping the family together.

As with any other relationship where trust has been broken, nothing starts the healing process more effectively than asking for forgiveness and apologizing for the mistakes you've made. Don't miss out on any opportunity to model forgiveness and reconciliation with your children. There are few things more powerful than having a humble parent kneel at their child's bedside, apologize, and ask for their forgiveness.

Treasuring Your Shared Past, Anticipating Your Shared Future

Although you can probably make a list of painful memories in your marriage that stretches for miles, you can rebuild trust by focusing on the memorable celebrations and favorite family events that are a part of your marriage history. For us, an important part of moving forward was to go back and revisit special places from our early years together, as well as to "reclaim" what the Enemy had stolen. We made a point of treasuring our shared past and focusing on the good things we remembered. For example, we revisited the marina where we were engaged in 1989. We had a great time talking about what happened that night, as well as all our lofty ideals and unrealistic expectations. Looking through old photographs and videos was another way we treasured our history.

In addition to revisiting fond memories from the past, we set a course to make new memories. Two years after we remarried, our church announced they were engaging in a makeover for a small church across the San Francisco Bay from where we lived. Being a part of that project gave us the chance to serve alongside each other in a new way. We made many friends during the project and the memory of our experience remains a highlight from the early years of our remarriage. Engaging in a family service project is another way to rebuild relationships between family members. Serving others also helps to take the focus of your circumstances and broadens your perspective.

Given our experience and those of the couples we've assisted, let us close this chapter by saying that, despite your best efforts, it's perfectly normal to experience trust "setbacks" from time-to-time. But, if you're both seeking God on a daily basis and being intentional about rebuilding trust, your relationship will grow and deepen. Exposing the ruins of betrayed trust to the light of Christ is critical for the health and restoration or your marriage. The same holds true for any trust setbacks that occur. Honestly acknowledge and confess your mistakes to God.

Finally, remember that in the process of rebuilding trust and dealing effectively with any setbacks, the emphasis must always be placed on *fact-finding*, not *fault-finding.* Like the archaeologist who gathers evidence to reconstruct events and make sense of them, you must keep the goal of learning from your mistakes and rebuilding trust at the forefront of your intentions. It is *never* appropriate to revisit the sins of the past in order to inflict pain or to open old wounds. Nothing will set your marriage back more quickly than engaging in this kind of unhealthy behavior. Instead, allow God to examine and restore broken trust from the past to positively impact your future. In the next chapter, we'll demonstrate effective ways to safeguard your marriage against betrayal and division from this day forward.

CHAPTER EXERCISES

Prayer to Rebuild Trust

Father, it is our desire to trust one another in a manner that communicates our love for You. In the past, we violated trust. And, there were times we didn't trust You. Forgive us and heal us where there are wounds from broken trust and intimacy. Rebuild on the ruins of our past. Show us how to trust one another and nurture trust in our marriage. Help us notice opportunities to demonstrate trust as well as to be vulnerable without a fear of rejection. Teach us to encourage trust in each other. Show us how to rebuild trust with our children and how to bring a sense of security to our family. Despite what has occurred, help us teach our children more about who You are. We pray that they would learn to trust You with their lives. Protect their vulnerabilities and help us to provide for their healing, as well as their physical, emotional, and spiritual needs. May our trust in You create greater intimacy in our marriage and strength in our family for Your glory. In Jesus' name. Amen.

Making Connections

Set aside uninterrupted time to discuss the specific things you can do for your spouse in order to nurture trust for him/her. Make note of your similarities and differences. Consider creating some key questions that you can ask each other when you need to have trust-building talks.

Scripture Reading
Reread Nehemiah 3 before answering the questions.

Questions to Consider

1. What is the hardest area of your life in which to trust God? How does God nurture trust with you? What convinces you to trust Him?

2. Do you consider yourself a trustworthy person? Give an example of a time when you were trustworthy in a difficult situation.

3. What are some specific steps you will take this week to nurture more trust in your marriage using the ideas from this chapter?

4. What did you notice about the manner in which Nehemiah proceeded in the rebuilding of Jerusalem's gates? How might this relate to restoring your marriage?

5. Take out your marriage timeline, add some blank paper to the right side of it, and extend the horizontal line. This will represent the future of your marriage and the clean slate you've been given by God. What hopes do you have regarding the future of your relationship?

Our current culture cultivates male/female relationships. Whether trust has been betrayed in the past or not, intentionally setting up a few safeguards can go a long way to protect your marriage from infidelity. Meeting alone with a person of the opposite sex can start out innocent, but we know how subtly a platonic relationship can turn into something neither person intended. Is it possible for men and women to "just be friends?" Of course it is. But an intimate friendship carries the risk of taking the road to something more. It's just the way we're wired.

The choice we've each made is to avoid putting ourselves in situations with someone of the opposite sex where an emotionally or physically intimate relationship could occur. Now, we don't go around policing each other where these safeguards are concerned. It's our responsibility to stand by these choices and fess up if we fall short. Clearly communicating these safeguards to our close friends has been important, too. Some people think we're a little paranoid about the agreements we've made with each other. We tell them if our decisions sound overly cautious, that's okay. Being considered silly or oversensitive is a price we're willing to pay to protect our marriage. After all, we know the cost of not doing so.

Gary and Mona Shriver
Founders of *Hope & Healing Ministries* and
Authors of *Unfaithful—Hope and Healing After Infidelity*
Denair, CA

Chapter 9 – Guarding the Gates of Marriage

*Then I said to them, "You see the trouble we are in:
Jerusalem lies in ruins, and its gates have been burned
with fire."*

Nehemiah 2:17

Enemy attacks were often concentrated at the gates of a
city because they were the most vulnerable points of
entry. Nehemiah's written account of Jerusalem's
restoration indicates that a great deal of the rebuilding process
had to do with making the necessary repairs to her gates, most of
which had been burned by fire. The third chapter of Nehemiah
contains a vivid description as to the labor and teamwork
necessary to completely restore the gates and set them in place.
According to biblical commentators, there were approximately
forty-five teams of workers on the wall, with at least forty
workers on each team. It is interesting to note that although the
division of roles and responsibilities between men and women
were distinct in those days, the great importance and urgency of
the task at hand allowed women and girls to participate in the
rebuilding (Nehemiah 3:12). Not only were females expected to
participate, but many people were required to labor outside of
their normal areas of expertise. For example, perfumers and
goldsmiths left the comfort zones of their intricate handiwork to
lift bulky building materials (Nehemiah 3:8).

During our trip to Israel, we had the opportunity to walk around each of the gates in modern-day Jerusalem. Not until years later did we realize how the restoration and historical significance of her gates, as well as Nehemiah's plan to guard them, directly applied to marriage. Each of Jerusalem's gates served an important purpose in the everyday operations of the city and each one serves an important illustration in the way marriage is intended to function. During this chapter, we invite you to join us on a tour of these gates, as they existed in Nehemiah's day. While commentators agree that these gates tell the Gospel story, they also provide an important analogy for maintaining a healthy and balanced marriage. Carefully guarding what each of these gates symbolizes will ensure the ongoing protection of your relationship.

During our counterclockwise tour (based on Nehemiah 3) we'll stop at each gate in order to apply its history and its significance to marriage. Don't hesitate to apply the things we'll share in this chapter to your relationship with your children, as well as to your marriage. Before we begin, it's important to note that we'll continue to use the *New International Version* of the Bible. Keep in mind that other translations may refer to these gates by different names. Their history, purpose, and symbolism, however, remain consistent in every version.

The Sheep Gate

> *Eliashib the high priest and his fellow priests went to work and rebuilt the Sheep Gate.*
>
> Nehemiah 3:1

The first gate we come to on our tour is the Sheep Gate which was located in the northeast corner of Jerusalem, near the Temple. It was through this gate that animals were brought to the Temple for sacrifice. It is no surprise that Eliashib and the other priests concentrated their work on this gate first, since it was their primary responsibility to enter the Temple and sacrifice animals to atone for the sins of the people.

In the New Testament, we read that Jesus Christ became the sacrifice for all our sins. *"The next day John saw Jesus coming toward him and said, 'Look, the Lamb of God, who takes away the sin of the world!'"* (John 1:29). Through Christ's redemptive work on the cross, our sins are forgiven and we're reconciled to God. When we're reconciled to God, we can be reconciled to one another.

Scholar and commentator J. Vernon McGee writes, "Personally, I think the Lord Jesus came in at the Sheep Gate every time he entered the city except for at the Triumphal Entry."[9] McGee goes on to speculate that Christ not only came in through the Sheep Gate, but when He was arrested and led out to be crucified, they took Him out through that gate as well.

In light of this information, the Sheep Gate speaks of several elements that are necessary for a healthy marriage. Of primary importance is the role of Christ in your relationship with your spouse (and your children). As stated earlier, we often remind couples that reconciliation is not about following a recipe, but about following Jesus Christ. He sacrificed His life for us, once and for all.

Guarding this area of your marriage and family means to be protective of the time you spend with God each day so that you remain reconciled to Him and stay in the center of His will. In addition, be mindful to keep Christ as the central focus of your marriage and family at all times. No person, possession, or responsibility should ever take precedence over your relationship with Him.

The Sheep Gate also reminds us that relationships demand self-sacrifice. Jesus stated in Luke 9:23, *"If anyone wishes to come after me, he must deny himself and take up his cross daily and follow me."* We are called to follow Christ's example. More than any other relationship ever created, marriage requires that you sacrifice your own desires and serve your spouse's needs before your own. I admit there are times when I'm selfish and must simply get on my face before God and repeat, "I choose You and I choose Clint." This phrase is my way of surrendering to God's desires and to serving Clint's needs before satisfying my own.

We encourage you to use a phrase of surrender or perhaps some visual image when faced with the struggle of sacrificing your own needs for God, your spouse, and/or your children. When you desire to have your way so badly that you can taste it, get on your knees and ask God to "feed" you with the bread of His presence.

During a recent marriage mission trip, God drove His point home in our hearts regarding the fact that marriage requires us to deny ourselves, whether we *feel* like it or not. Near the end of the journey we'd grown very weary of life on the road. Being away from home and traveling together for forty days has its challenges and it's easy to become lax in serving each other. On this particular afternoon, we happened to be driving down a lonely highway in Louisiana when, suddenly, Clint blurted out, "Look, there's Jesus!" Off in the distance was a long-haired man, dressed in a white robe. We both blinked our eyes in disbelief. As we got closer, we could see that the man dressed like Jesus was dragging a huge cross down the side of the highway. As we passed him in our van, he raised his hand and called out, "God bless you!"

Seeing him drag that heavy cross down that road etched the reality of what Jesus requires into our minds in a way we won't soon forget. No doubt, your marriage and relationships with other family members will require frequent stops at the Sheep Gate to remember the incredible sacrifice that Jesus—the spotless Lamb of God—made for you.

The Fish Gate

> *The Fish Gate was rebuilt by the sons of Hassenaah. They laid its beams and put its doors and bolts and bars in place.*
>
> Nehemiah 3:3

As we continue our walk around the northern wall of the city, we come to the Fish Gate. Through this gate, merchants brought in their catch from the Mediterranean, the Sea of Galilee, the Jordan River, and other nearby waters. The Fish Gate symbolizes the call of Jesus to His disciples. Matthew 4:19 reads, *"Come, follow me," Jesus said, "and I will make you fishers of men."* Once we're saved to eternal life, we're expected to be witnesses of God's love to the rest of the world.

It was through the love of several married couples that I (Penny) was wooed back into the folds of the faith many years ago. These couples, whom I met through my job as a school principal, tenderly took me under their wings and loved me, despite the mistakes I'd made in the past. They had no idea how closely I was observing their interactions with each other and their relationships with their kids. Through the witness of these families, I was drawn into a more authentic relationship with Christ.

183

Your marriage has the potential to be a powerful witness. One of the ways you can "fish" for men and women to come to faith in Christ is through the witness of a restored marriage. Your children, family, friends, and other people in your sphere of influence are all impacted by your marriage story and you are one of the determining factors as to whether that impact is positive or negative.

If you think people aren't watching your marriage, think again. Being mindful to guard this gate means that, at *all* times, you're aware of what your marriage says about God to those around you. It's imperative that you regularly reflect at the Fish Gate and ask, "What does our marriage say about God to those who are watching us? How can we strengthen our witness for Christ through our marriage? In what ways can our family be an effective witness of God's love and desire to heal others?"

The Jeshanah Gate

> *The Jeshanah Gate was repaired by Joiada son of Paseah and Meshullam son of Besodeiah. They laid its beams and put its doors and bolts and bars in place.*
>
> Nehemiah 3:6

The Jeshanah Gate is also referred to as the Old Gate. The application of this gate to marriage is best explained by the following verse from the book of Jeremiah: *"This is what the LORD says: 'Stand at the crossroads and look, ask for the ancient paths, ask where the good way is, and walk in it, and you will find rest for your souls.' But you said, 'We will not walk in it'"* (Jeremiah 6:16).

Many marriage troubles occur because one or both spouses aren't focused on being a disciple of Christ as their *first* priority. The rising rate of divorce in the church is evidence of our need to get back to the basics of our Christian faith. Become an avid student of discipleship and marriage. Study the people whose relationships with God you admire. One of the best ways to do this is to ask people who've been following God a long time how they continue to grow in their relationships with Him, with their spouses, and with their children. Learn about the things others do to strengthen those relationships. Observe the interactions of couples or families you respect and don't be afraid to ask them for help or advice.

Several of the ministries with whom we link arms across the nation are passionate about integrating marriage mentoring as an essential thread in the fabric of their churches. In Rutland, Vermont, for example, a team of pastors and their wives have banded together to implement a large-scale marriage mentoring program that spans across ten different churches in their community. The goal is to have every couple in need appropriately matched with a mature mentor couple who will meet regularly to help them over any hurdles they encounter.

Over the course of our remarriage, we've had several mentor couples who have provided us with wise counsel. The lessons we've learned from them have proven to be a resource on which we continually draw. These folks also keep us on the up and up in all areas of our lives.

What we've discovered over the years is that, for the most part, couples who've been through the fire will benefit most from having a mentor couple who has also been through the fire, sifted through the ashes, and has risen together to heal. Can you think of a couple right now who might serve as your marriage mentors? We encourage you to make a list of potential couples

185

and/or to begin asking God for a mature couple who will be a regular resource and sounding board for you. Mentors should be well-grounded in the faith and have a strong individual relationship with God. Guarding this marriage gate means that you maintain a high regard for seeking counsel from those who have walked the narrow road of marriage before you.

The Valley Gate

> *The Valley Gate was repaired by Hanun and the residents of Zanoah. They rebuilt it and put its doors and bolts and bars in place.*
>
> Nehemiah 3:13

The Valley Gate leads us out of the city and down into the surrounding valley. This gate served as a perpetual reminder of one of the darkest times in Israel's history. During the period when the children of disobedient Israelites were sacrificed to worship the pagan god, Molech, they were led through the Valley Gate to meet their deaths.[10]

No doubt you're well-acquainted with the struggles inherent in a valley or you wouldn't be reading this book. Spiritual valleys are those places you'll routinely travel as long as you're living on this side of heaven. Sometimes our valleys—like those of the Israelites—are a result of disobedience and sin. Sometimes, they're a result of someone else's poor choices. Valleys and suffering are also an important part of the supernatural way God refines His children. Whatever the reason for a valley, keep in mind that the Enemy also longs to use it for a much different purpose: to distract you from your relationship with God and to divide your marriage. Standing guard at the Valley Gate means that you take all necessary precautions not to fall prey to the doubt, discouragement, or disillusionment that looms in the valley when your eyes aren't firmly fixed on God.

All the great saints of the faith were familiar with seasons of suffering. In the Gospel of John, Jesus plainly stated, *"In this world you will have trouble. But take heart! I have overcome the world"* (John 16:33). Reflecting at the Valley Gate reminds you that there will continue to be difficulties during your marriage journey. There will be times when you're both faced with a dip into the valley through an external circumstance such as a death of a friend. Or, you might experience a low in your lives due to an internal crisis such as unresolved feelings from your past or a setback during the restoration of your marriage. When events of this nature occur, you must join together as husband and wife and ask God to use your circumstances to knit you together even more tightly.

In the valley, there are days when one of you will feel stronger than the other. One season, you'll take care of your spouse. The next season, it will be your spouse's turn to tend to your needs. The important thing is to lean into God together all the way through the experiences and pray that your hearts remain steadfast and faithful. Be intentional about asking God for ways to stick closely to one another despite the difficulties you're experiencing.

You may also find that you enter a valley at a different time than your spouse does. For example, when we moved from California to Florida in 2007, Clint was on top of the world. He longed to return to Florida where he'd lived prior to our remarriage, and he was excited about our new adventure. I, on the other hand, wrestled with *every* aspect of our relocation. While Clint celebrated and embraced the change, I grieved over the loss of everything familiar, including family and friends. Although we both believed our move was orchestrated by God and we agreed on the move together, more than four decades of deeply planted roots in the California soil made transplanting to the east coast one of the hardest things God has ever required of me.

Had Clint and I not been intentional about recognizing the differences in how we viewed and coped with the move, it could have had a devastating impact on our marriage. Although Clint wasn't walking through the valley, he supported me and was patient in giving me the freedom to do what I needed to do in order to adjust. In a very real way, Clint stood guard at the Valley Gate on my behalf, observing and supporting my every step by choosing to walk beside me long after the boxes were unpacked. His faithfulness and courage was a tangible demonstration of his love for me, even though he felt very differently about our relocation and didn't completely understand my feelings.

Whether just one of you is struggling, or you find yourselves dipping into the valley together, remember that your journey requires humility before God and each other at all times. Humility indicates that you have an accurate view of who God is, who you are, and who you are becoming as *one flesh* through the valley experience. There are no short cuts to the lessons God will teach you during tough times but, as you learn to be humble, a valley will undeniably deepen the intimacy in your marriage.

The Dung Gate

> *The Dung Gate was repaired by Malkijah son of Recab, ruler of the district of Beth Hakkerem. He rebuilt it and put its doors and bolts and bars in place.*
>
> Nehemiah 3:14

It's probably safe to assume that because of its name, you already have an idea of the Dung Gate's purpose. Located at the southwest angle of Mt. Zion, the city's garbage and refuse was taken out of this gate each evening. Getting rid of this waste on a daily basis was critical to the health of the entire city.

In marriage, you are wise to revisit the significance of the Dung Gate many times during a given day! Subtle sins can quickly enter into the human heart if you do not symbolically guard this gate by giving God free reign to cleanse out the gunky build-up. *"If we confess our sins, he is faithful and just and will forgive us our sins and purify us from all unrighteousness"* (1 John 1:9).

One of the things that initially attracted me to Clint the second time around was how humbly he confessed the sins of his past. Later, I discovered he'd been attracted to me for the very same reason. When God intersected our lives again, we were totally honest about all the mistakes we'd made along the way. *"He who conceals his sins does not prosper, but whoever confesses and renounces them finds mercy"* (Proverbs 28:13).

As stated in a previous chapter, we cannot stress enough how essential it is to come before God in regular times of confession and forgiveness. The overall health of your marriage and family will quickly grow sour if you neglect coming before God each day with an honest admission of your sins and shortcomings. The foot of the cross is the only place to get rid of the excess waste our hearts collect during a given day. It's never fun to admit that you're wrong, especially to your spouse. However, we've discovered that more than any other aspect of our relationship, complete honesty never fails to enrich our marriage, no matter how difficult it may be to get the words out or fess up to our mistakes.

The Fountain Gate

The Fountain Gate was repaired by Shallun son of Col-Hozeh, ruler of the district of Mizpah. He rebuilt it, roofing it over and putting its doors and bolts and bars in place. He also repaired the wall of the Pool of Siloam, by the King's Garden, as far as the steps going down from the City of David.

Nehemiah 3:15

The Fountain Gate was most likely located on the southeastern wall of the city, next to the royal gardens of the king. Its location allowed for the irrigation of these gardens so the vineyards and plants would grow, its fruits would ripen, and its full beauty could be displayed.

Symbolically, the Fountain Gate represents the filling of the Holy Spirit—a fountain that must continually flow in all our relationships. It was at the Feast of the Tabernacles that Christ stood up and declared,

"If anyone is thirsty, let him come to me and drink. Whoever believes in me, as the Scripture has said, streams of living water will flow from within him." By this he meant the Spirit, whom those who believed in him were later to receive. Up to that time the Spirit had not been given, since Jesus had not yet been glorified.

John 7:37–39

Each morning before I (Clint) begin reading my Bible, I specifically ask God to fill me with the Holy Spirit. I shudder to think about entering a day without drinking deeply of the Holy

Spirit's life-giving fountain. Being filled is essential for the growth of my relationship with God and my marriage.

In his book, *Living in the Power of the Holy Spirit,* Charles Stanley writes, "Every day, ask the Holy Spirit to fill your life anew with His life-giving, joy producing, comforting, guiding, renewing presence. Every day, ask the Holy Spirit to fill you anew with His love, His peace, His truth. Every day, ask the Holy Spirit to fill you to overflowing with His compassion for others."[11]

Because of Christ's reconciling work on the cross, we have access to an unlimited resource of power, wisdom, and love through the indwelling Holy Spirit. This is the same Spirit present in the apostles and prophets of long ago. Consider all the wonders and miracles performed through these men and women of the faith. The same powerful Holy Spirit lives in you if you've taken Christ as your Savior and Lord.

The ongoing restoration of your marriage is fueled and fed by the Holy Spirit who is alive and working in your heart at every moment. Tap into His fountain! Guard this gate with passion! Ask the Holy Spirit to nudge you when you're walking a fine line or are tempted to repeat an old pattern in your marriage. Be zealous for more and more of the Holy Spirit and your marriage will overflow with the infinite attributes of God. Observe the working of the Holy Spirit in the lives of other believers. Ask God to increase both the measure and the manifestation of the Spirit in your life.

The Water Gate

> *And the temple servants living on the hill of Ophel made repairs up to a point opposite the Water Gate toward the east and the projecting tower.*
>
> Nehemiah 3:26

At this point on our tour, we find ourselves in front of the Water Gate. Historically, only a portion of the city's water flowed into Jerusalem through a series of skillfully constructed aqueducts. The remainder of the water was hand-carried through the Water Gate. As you may have guessed, this gate represents God's Word.

Notice that in the book of Nehemiah there's no mention of any repairs being made to this gate. Of all ten gates, the Water Gate is the only one that remained fully intact during the siege. This fact speaks volumes about the holy and infallible nature of the Bible. Through God's perfect Word, we're cleansed from all our imperfections and presented blameless before Him.

> *Wives, submit to your husbands as to the Lord. For the husband is the head of the wife as Christ is the head of the church, his body, of which he is the Savior. Now as the church submits to Christ, so also wives should submit to their husbands in everything. Husbands, love your wives, just as Christ loved the church and gave himself up for her to make her holy, cleansing her by the washing with water through the word, and to present her to himself as a radiant church, without stain or wrinkle or any other blemish, but holy and blameless.*
>
> Ephesians 5:22–27

Many years ago, when our pastor finally found out our marriage was in crisis, he confronted us using this passage from Ephesians. At that point, I (Penny) already had one foot out the door and vehemently disagreed with anything and everything he said. I didn't understand the cyclical nature of the *mutual* submission described in this passage, mostly because I didn't

192

want to. My heart had grown hard and cold. I was no longer guarding over my time in the Word. Eventually, I stopped reading it altogether. Closing my Bible, my heart, and my mind allowed the Enemy to ravage our marriage.

As stated in the Chapter 3 of *Marriage on the Mend*, it's easy to let other things crowd out the time we should spend reading and studying God's Word. That's why it's necessary to guard this gate by carving out your time with God as a non-negotiable part of your day. Give someone permission to hold you accountable to your commitment of reading and applying the Scriptures to your life. Taking God at His word and getting the Bible into every crack and crevasse of your heart is a lifelong pursuit worthy of your time and effort. Meditating on and memorizing verses from the Bible will also help keep your marriage in the center of God's will. You will get out of God's Word what you put into it. The rewards and benefits far outweigh any costs.

The Horse Gate

Above the Horse Gate, the priests made repairs, each in front of his own house.

Nehemiah 3:28

Our next stop is the Horse Gate, located at the easternmost point in the wall. Scholars note that men rode horses only during times of war. Consequently, armies rode into battle through this gate. There's no doubt that the Horse Gate speaks of the spiritual battles you've faced and will continue to face until you reach heaven.

Finally, be strong in the Lord and in his mighty power. Put on the full armor of God so that you can take your stand against the devil's schemes. For our struggle is not against flesh and blood, but against the rulers, against the authorities, against the powers of this dark world and against the spiritual forces of evil in the heavenly realms. Therefore put on the full armor of God, so that when the day of evil comes, you may be able to stand your ground, and after you have done everything, to stand.

Ephesians 6:10–13

You've probably discerned by now that we were immature in our faith when we were married the first time. We had no idea how desperately the Enemy wanted to destroy our union. He went to great lengths to pull us apart, and his appetite to take down marriages is only gaining momentum in these latter days. Be absolutely certain of this: staying married means you'll have a fight on your hands. But remember, you are rising *together* to fight against the *real* Enemy, not against each another.

Standing guard at the Horse Gate means that, through prayer, you dress your marriage each day in the spiritual armor God has given you to wage this war (Ephesians 6:14–17). Not only must you clothe your marriage in God's spiritual armor each day, but through prayer, clothe your children as well. Your children are the fruit of your marriage and that fruit must have God's protection as it blossoms, grows, and ripens.

One of the ways we dress our marriage in God's spiritual armor is by reaching out to each other while we're still in bed, and praying silently for God's blessing, covering, and protection. Visualize each part of God's armor being placed on your spouse from head-to-toe as you pray. To clothe your children in God's spiritual armor, you can do something similar at their bedsides or in the doorway of their bedrooms as they sleep.

The East Gate

> *Next to them, Zadok son of Immer made repairs opposite his house. Next to him, Shemaiah son of Shecaniah, the guard at the East Gate, made repairs. Next to him, Hananiah son of Shelemiah, and Hanun, the sixth son of Zalaph, repaired another section. Next to them, Meshullam son of Berekiah made repairs opposite his living quarters.*
>
> Nehemiah 3:29–30

Facing in the direction of the rising sun, the East Gate was the first gate opened each morning. The watchmen who were set in place to guard this gate walked back and forth, making their rounds and keeping a keen eye on the city until the first light of day. In modern-day Jerusalem, the East Gate remains sealed because some believe it is the Golden Gate through which Christ will return. However, many other scholars say the East Gate is just a predecessor to the Golden Gate through which Jesus will one day enter.

Despite this debate, we can be fully confident that the East Gate symbolizes the ever-present hope we have in Christ. In the same manner the watchmen and gatekeepers waited for the dawning of a new day, we keep watch and await the second coming of Jesus Christ. *"Because of the tender mercy of our God, by which the rising sun will come to us from heaven to shine on those living in darkness and in the shadow of death, to guide our feet into the path of peace"* (Luke 1:78–79).

Each month, we receive countless calls and e-mails from abandoned spouses who have lost all hope that their marriages can be restored. While we offer them encouragement, we also know that we cannot guarantee that their spouses will return. What we can promise is the hope they have in a God who will never leave them hanging. *"May the God of hope fill you with all joy and peace as you trust in him, so that you may overflow with hope by the power of the Holy Spirit"* (Romans 15:13).

One of the highlights from a recent mission trip was an evening we spent with twelve men in West Nyack, New York, who are all hoping together for the reconciliation of their marriages. We were humbled as each guy around the table shared his struggles and doubts. One of the men, who has become very dear to our hearts, said it best. "Divorce is the pain that never goes away."

Dennis is right. The pain of divorce never leaves, but neither does the hope these men are clinging to in Christ! All of these guys are hoping for a second chance with their wives and we pray that one day, they will each receive it. Until then, these brothers have decided to band together in order to be a source of encouragement and hope to each other. As we parted ways, we reminded them that a long, long time ago, twelve godly men turned the world upside-down, all because their hopes were set on Jesus Christ.

You have a second chance. Don't ever take that second chance for granted! The East Gate symbolizes the new mercy you can claim as you arise and start each day. Someone once said that Christ has turned every sunset into a new dawn. Until you reach heaven, you'll be in the process of restoring your marriage. You'll experience set-backs and make mistakes. We do, too. But, we also know that Christ offers His hope to us each morning and we have the privilege of receiving and extending that same hope to one another.

The Inspection Gate

Next to him, Malkijah, one of the goldsmiths, made repairs as far as the house of the temple servants and the merchants, opposite the Inspection Gate, and as far as the room above the corner.

Nehemiah 3:31

At the conclusion of a battle, soldiers re-entered the city through the Inspection Gate. Here, the king would be present to review and inspect his troops. Many times, King David examined the state of his warriors at this gate as they returned from battle. In addition, strangers entering the city had to stop at the Inspection Gate and register their presence; a modern-day equivalent of obtaining a visa.

In regard to its application for marriage, the Inspection Gate speaks of the account we, as believers, are expected to give to God regarding our deeds and words. *"It is written: 'As surely as I live' says the Lord, 'every knee will bow before me; every tongue will confess to God.' So then, each of us will give an account of himself to God"* (Romans 14:11–12).

As Christians, not only are we accountable to God, but we're also expected to be accountable to our spouses and other brothers and sisters in Christ. Accountability in your relationships with others simply means that you intentionally ask a few people that you trust to check-up on your spiritual growth. For example, we both have prayer partners. These folks are given full access to our lives and permission to provide us with feedback and correction as to our spiritual development and the

197

status of our marriage. Being held accountable to the standards in God's Word and the standards in your marriage are essential parts of understanding God's plan for you and maintaining the courage to stick to that plan. We never had accountability or prayer partners in our first marriage, but the second time around, this is a non-negotiable standard. (Accountability/prayer partners will be discussed in greater detail in Chapter 10.)

In addition to having accountability/prayer partners, a stop at the Inspection Gate means that you sit quietly before God on a regular basis and ask His Holy Spirit to examine your heart for impure motives, negative thoughts, sins, and other things that do not please Him. One practical way of doing this is to picture your heart as a house with many rooms; such as a library, bedroom, kitchen, living room, garage, game room, attic, basement, etc. Ask the Holy Spirit to walk with you through each room and examine it for things that aren't pleasing to God. For example, in the game room, ask Him if all the ways you entertain yourself edify Him, including the television shows and movies you watch and Internet sites you surf. In the basement, ask Him to inspect all the things you may have unknowingly stored in your heart such as bitterness or unforgiveness.

A powerful extension of this kind of heart inspection is to engage in it with your spouse. This may take some practice, but this kind of regular room-by-room inspection allows God to have full access to every part of your individual hearts and the heart of your marriage.

Coming Full Circle

And between the room above the corner and the Sheep Gate the goldsmiths and merchants made repairs.

Nehemiah 3:32

We conclude our tour of Jerusalem's gates right back where we started; at the Sheep Gate. What could be more appropriate? Coming back around to this gate symbolizes that Jesus Christ must be both the beginning and the end of every aspect of your marriage. As husbands and wives, *everything* you do and say must begin and end at the cross.

Pause and reflect at the Sheep Gate, asking God whether or not *every* aspect of your marriage (behaviors, attitudes, actions, language, and so forth) is completely encircled within His will at *all* times. Be still and quiet before Him. Shut every other voice out except for God's. Allow the price He paid to purchase your redemption to deeply penetrate your heart. Do you truly realize that you were the joy set before Christ when He endured the cross and sacrificed His life? Do you set His joy before you when serving your spouse and family?

Being a Marriage Gatekeeper

After the wall had been rebuilt and I had set the doors in place, the gatekeepers and the singers and the Levites were appointed. I put in charge of Jerusalem my brother Hanani, along with Hananiah the commander of the citadel, because he was a man of integrity and feared God more than most men do. I said to them, "The gates of Jerusalem are not to be opened until the sun is hot. While the gatekeepers are still on duty, have them shut the doors and bar them. Also appoint residents of Jerusalem as guards, some at their posts and some near their own houses."

Nehemiah 7:1–3

To conclude our tour, let's visually summarize the symbolism for marriage found at each of the ten gates.

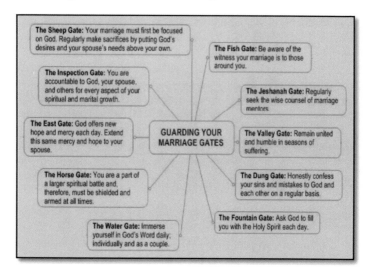

The Sheep Gate: Your marriage must first be focused on God. Regularly make sacrifices by putting God's desires and your spouse's needs above your own.

The Fish Gate: Be aware of the witness your marriage is to those around you.

The Inspection Gate: You are accountable to God, your spouse, and others for every aspect of your spiritual and marital growth.

The Jeshanah Gate: Regularly seek the wise counsel of marriage mentors.

The East Gate: God offers new hope and mercy each day. Extend this same mercy and hope to your spouse.

GUARDING YOUR MARRIAGE GATES

The Valley Gate: Remain united and humble in seasons of suffering.

The Horse Gate: You are a part of a larger spiritual battle and, therefore, must be shielded and armed at all times.

The Dung Gate: Honestly confess your sins and mistakes to God and each other on a regular basis.

The Water Gate: Immerse yourself in God's Word daily; individually and as a couple.

The Fountain Gate: Ask God to fill you with the Holy Spirit each day.

Immediately after the gates were repaired and put back into place, Nehemiah set up a system of ongoing protection and defense over these vulnerable entry points. The gates of the city were shut and barred at the close of each day by the city's gatekeepers. In addition, Nehemiah instructed the gatekeepers not to open the gates at the first light of day as had been their custom. Commentators reason that Nehemiah gave these instructions to prevent Jerusalem's enemies from launching a surprise attack at the gates during the early morning hours when people were still asleep.

We also see from this passage that Nehemiah chose reputable people to guard the city and keep watch over its gates. Posting people to stand guard near their homes also demonstrated Nehemiah's knowledge of the human psyche; namely, that we are much more apt to guard well the things that are close to the territory most dear to our hearts.

Becoming a marriage gatekeeper is part of your responsibility to God and to your spouse. It's imperative to keep a careful watch over the health and balance in your relationship by regularly reflecting and inspecting the areas of your marriage that each gate symbolizes. You may have noticed that not every gate in Jerusalem was in the same state of disrepair. Some gates required more work than others, but because they each served an important purpose, they had to be completely repaired and then, carefully guarded.

There will be times where the same will be said for your marriage. The Holy Spirit will help you detect the places in your relationship that are still vulnerable or in need of a little work. From time to time, you'll be required to make these repairs in order to be sure all your marriage gates are set in place and functioning in the way that God intends. In the next chapter, we'll discuss the ways you can gain a greater awareness of the specific opponents and attacks that may pose a threat to your marriage gates and how you, like Nehemiah, can actively apply tools and strategies to ensure the ongoing stability of your relationship.

CHAPTER EXERCISES

Prayer to Guard the Gates of Your Marriage

God, we want to protect the spiritual gates of our marriage. Help us remember that our relationship begins and ends with You. Remind us not to put anyone or anything in Your place. Show us new ways to follow Your example by sacrificing our desires and focusing on meeting each other's needs first. We want our marriage to reflect You to those who gather around us. Give us opportunities to witness to others through our marriage and family. We admit that we don't have all the answers. Provide us with marriage mentors and other spiritually mature couples who can help us protect our marriage and keep it growing. When trials come, show us how to walk through the valleys together. May we learn to follow Your example of humility in the face of suffering. Remind us to come to You and admit our sins on a daily basis. Grant us repentant hearts that seek and extend forgiveness. Fill us with an overflowing measure of Your Holy Spirit each day as we spend time in Your Word. Arm and equip us with everything we need to fight the battles we'll face. Clothe us in Your spiritual armor. Let not the Enemy discourage or distract us. Instead, let us fix our eyes on You as our hope. Holy Spirit, hold us accountable to the things You require of us. Guard each of the gates of our marriage and show us how to keep watch over the things that matter most. In Jesus' name. Amen.

Making Connections

Illustrate a simple map of each of the ten gates of Jerusalem and what they represent in marriage (such as the diagram found on page 200). Next to each gate, write one idea or tool you will implement to help you guard what that gate symbolizes in your marriage.

Scripture Reading

Review Nehemiah 4 and read Chapters 5 and 6 before answering the questions.

Questions to Consider

1. What do you consider to be the spiritual gates in your marriage that are in the greatest need of repair?

2. How can you apply the symbolism of each of the ten gates to your relationship with your children?

3. In your review of Chapters Nehemiah 4-6, what kind of opposition does he seem to face and what do you notice about the way he wards off his enemies?

4. As you look back over your marriage timeline, can you identify the places or times where certain gates were left unguarded?

Marv and I were married for more than twenty years when our marriage drifted into crisis, and we were separated for three long years before God reconciled our relationship.

At first, getting back together was scary because we were afraid of falling back into old habits. Thankfully, others came beside us to give us guidance, and we each met with people who kept us accountable. To this day, Marv continues to participate in a men's accountability group begun during that time. In addition, keeping in close contact with each other throughout the day helped us restore trust and closeness.

An essential part of our moving forward was reading the Bible together daily for the first year and then continuing to have our individual devotional times with prayer and Bible reading after that. We keep on nourishing our marriage by going out almost every weekend just to enjoy each other's company. Most importantly, we've both made changes in the way we deal with our relationship. I am more watchful of my words and the things I say, and Marv is careful to resolve conflicts when they arise so they don't fester and get away from us. I make an effort to show Marv my appreciation, and he supports me around the house.

These are the changes we each needed to make to help heal our marriage for a lifetime. No matter how much time passes, we are aware of the need to keep growing together and to watch out for pitfalls that might cause a slide backwards into bad habits.

Linda Rooks
Author of *Broken Heart on Hold—Surviving Separation*
Maitland, FL

Chapter 10 – Retrofitting Your Relationship

aving lived in California for most of our lives, we are well acquainted with the earthquakes and aftershocks common there. When the Loma Prieta quake struck in 1989, we'd been married for just over a month. Many structures suffered major damage, and government agencies launched widespread efforts to inspect and retrofit unstable buildings, highways, and bridges. For those of you unfamiliar with the term, a *retrofit* allows for the modification of existing structures in order to make them more resistant to damage caused by seismic activity. Perhaps if we'd known how to retrofit our young marriage with tools such as the ones in this chapter, we would have had a better chance of surviving the major shake-ups in our relationship.

Like an earthquake, you never know when great difficulty may strike the heart of your marriage and threaten its sustainability. The focus of this chapter is to learn how to stabilize your marriage from the sudden jolts and aftershocks that occur as you continue your journey together. Regularly guarding your marriage gates, inspecting the vulnerable places in your relationship where damage is likely to occur, and shoring up any instability will ensure that—no matter what strikes—your marriage will remain standing long after disaster has passed.

Up until this point in *Marriage on the Mend,* many of the tools we've given you have been *reactive* (tools to use in the midst of, or after the crisis). In this chapter, however, we'll provide you with several *proactive* measures to be used on a regular basis so that your relationship remains stable amidst life's ups and downs. We'll also present several tools to help you work together as a team to defend and fortify your marriage. Utilizing a balance of reactive *and* proactive tools will make your marriage more resilient.

In addition to these proactive tools, through our continued study of Nehemiah, we'll identify the types of opposition and trouble he faced and the wise strategies that were deployed to meet his enemies head on and defeat them.

Before we begin, we ask you to keep in mind the letter we wrote as the introduction to this book. If necessary, reread it. We mention this letter to remind you, once again, of a crucial mistake spouses often make: fighting against each other instead of rising up against the real Enemy. Your spouse is your ally, not your enemy, and uniting to face any and all opponents will separate a weak marriage from a strong one.

Identifying Your Opponents *and* Their Tactics

You know by now that, as the wall around Jerusalem was being restored, Nehemiah encountered relentless opposition. Found in many chapters of the book bearing his name is a vast collection of evidence proving Nehemiah had a nasty fight on his hands. Listed below are just some of his enemy's tactics to stop the process of restoration and rebuilding.

Ridicule, mocking, humiliation, anger, and sarcasm:

> *When Sanballat heard that we were rebuilding the wall, he became angry and was greatly incensed. He ridiculed the Jews, and in the presence of his associates and the army of Samaria, he said, "What are those feeble Jews doing? Will they restore their wall? Will they offer sacrifices? Will they finish in a day? Can they bring the stones back to life from those heaps of rubble—burned as they are?"*
>
> Nehemiah 4:1–2

Taunts and scheming:

> *Sanballat and Geshem sent me this message: "Come, let us meet together in one of the villages on the plain of Ono." But they were scheming to harm me.*
>
> Nehemiah 6:2

Playing on inadequacies and weaknesses:

> *Tobiah the Ammonite, who was at his side, said, "What they are building—if even a fox climbed up on it, he would break down their wall of stones!"*
>
> Nehemiah 4:3

Fear and intimidation:

> *They were all trying to frighten us, thinking, "Their hands will get too weak for the work, and it will not be completed."*
>
> Nehemiah 6:9

Slander:

> *He had been hired to intimidate me so that I would commit a sin by doing this, and then they would give me a bad name to discredit me.*
>
> Nehemiah 6:13

Satan possessed a wide variety of weapons in his arsenal back then and, unfortunately, he still does today. Many of his schemes are precisely and relentlessly targeted to destroy marriages and families. However, we know that the ultimate victor in this battle has already been determined. Because of Christ's death on the cross and resurrection from the grave, you can trust God to use every bit of the opposition you encounter for a heavenly purpose. When your challenges are handled in a way that honors God, they can actually serve to retrofit your marriage.

It's important to note that some of the opposition Nehemiah faced was *internal* and some of it was *external.* In the Bible passages listed so far in this chapter, his opposition was external. In other words, problems were coming at Nehemiah from sources outside the walls of the city. Sanballat, Geshem, and Tobiah were three troublemakers who relentlessly stirred up problems in an attempt to overthrow Nehemiah's efforts. More specifically, Sanballat and his allies viewed Nehemiah as a political threat. Jerusalem had been lying in ruins for 150 years. Until Nehemiah arrived on the scene, all other attempts to rebuild the city had been aborted. Nehemiah's presence, power, and influence over the people now posed a political threat that ruffled the feathers of his opponents in a major way.

A careful study of other passages from Nehemiah also reveals that some of his opposition was *internal.* In other words, the workers who were supposed to be supporting the rebuilding efforts created some of Nehemiah's most monumental problems.

The following passages are just two examples of the internal opposition he encountered.

Discouragement and weariness among the laborers:

> *Meanwhile, the people in Judah said, "The strength of the laborers is giving out, and there is so much rubble that we cannot rebuild the wall."*
>
> Nehemiah 4:10

Arguments and complaints against one another:

> *Now the men and their wives raised a great outcry against their Jewish brothers. Some were saying, "We and our sons and daughters are numerous; in order for us to eat and stay alive, we must get grain." Others were saying, "We are mortgaging our fields, our vineyards and our homes to get grain during the famine." Still others were saying, "We have had to borrow money to pay the king's tax on our fields and vineyards."*
>
> Nehemiah 5:1–4

Like Nehemiah, you've undoubtedly encountered both *internal* and *external* opposition in your marriage. To some degree, you will face opposition in the future as well. Examples of internal opposition may be things such as a spouse who is battling a life-threatening illness or a prodigal son/daughter who wanders from the family. Examples of external opposition may be things such as a downturn in the economy, a meddling co-worker, or an argument with a friend.

Regardless of whether his opponents came from inside or outside Jerusalem's walls, Nehemiah knew who and what he was dealing with at all times. He maintained an awareness that the work they were engaged in would come under fire and he planned accordingly. Someone once said that a chain is only as strong as its weakest link. Nehemiah's actions prove that he was an advocate of this truth. He carefully organized the workers along the wall in order to secure that equal progress was being made on all sides and that no part the city was left defenseless.[12]

So we rebuilt the wall till all of it reached half its height, for the people worked with all their heart.

Nehemiah 4:6

Coming at Us from All Sides

An example of *internal* opposition in our restoration occurred about a year after we remarried. I'd (Penny) accepted a promotion to a new administrative position in our school district. To celebrate, we decided to go waterskiing. During the last run of the day, I injured my back as the boat jerked me up out of the water. As a result of the injury, I had to leave my job and the school district I'd worked in for thirteen years.

In an instant, our whole lives were turned upside-down. I struggled with not being able to work, do household chores, or much of anything else. The accident impacted our finances and our marriage in major ways. However, soon after, we made a conscious decision to ask God to use what had happened for good purposes. As difficult as the physical pain was (and still is) and the impact all of this had on our marriage, it was comforting and inspiring to see how God met us and led us at every turn.

Now, as we look back on all the incredible experiences that came as a result of God's sovereignty, we stand amazed. What could have taken our marriage down became the very thing that strengthened it. (More of this life-changing journey can be read about in the book, *The Path of Most Resistance—A True Story of Reconciliation and Hope*[13]).

One example of *external* opposition we faced occurred at Clint's school. As word of our unique reconciliation spread, we were asked to share our story on a Christian television program. During our interview, we candidly discussed the affair that ended our first marriage. A few days later, the producer of the segment placed the script from our story on the Internet. We never thought much more about it, until months later when one of Clint's middle school students came across our story and spread word of my affair around the school.

Serving as a volunteer in Clint's classroom at the time, I'd gotten to know many of his students and happened to be present the day the matter came to Clint's attention. I watched as a young man approached him after class and confessed that for several days, he'd been spreading the website and my affair around the whole school. Evidently, after he'd hyped up his classmates, he felt guilty for his actions and wanted to come clean.

"Mr. Bragg," the young man began…nervously scuffing his shoes against the gym floor. "I just wanted to tell you that I read all about you and your wife on the Internet and spread it around the whole school. I'm sorry."

Although we knew our story was becoming more public and we had agreed to expose our scars to help others, we were unprepared for the emotions and feelings that would accompany the exposure, especially at this level. What the student did hit me hard. Ashamed, I hated to think Clint would be encountering problems at school because of my indiscretion years earlier.

Clint could have easily gotten bitter toward me and become embarrassed by what was being spread around. Instead, he responded to the young man with a dignity I'll never forget. He placed his hand on the student's shoulder, looked him squarely in the eyes and said, "Son, thank you for telling me what you did. I accept your apology. My wife and I have nothing to hide."

Without even having the time to figure out a response together, Clint united us as husband and wife. With that one simple response, we joined forces right in the middle of the unexpected external opposition.

Take a moment right now and think about one trial or difficulty you're facing. Is it coming from inside your marriage or from an outside source? It may sound strange but, oftentimes, half the battle is identifying the nature of the attack. We often ask God to "expose the truth of our circumstances," so we can really see what we're dealing with. Sometimes after we've prayed, waited, and searched the Scriptures, He'll reveal the nature of the opposition that couldn't be seen at the onset.

Once you accurately identify whether each struggle you're facing is internal or external, make a conscious decision to unite as a team and ask God for a plan to meet that specific form of opposition. Maintain an awareness that you can't let down your defenses toward the real Enemy. Be mindfully aware that he doesn't want your marriage to make it. Whatever the case, agree to face your trials together and hold each other accountable to your agreement. Leaving your mate stranded to do battle alone is *never* an option.

Posting a Guard

> *So we rebuilt the wall till all of it reached half its height, for the people worked with all their heart. But when Sanballat, Tobiah, the Arabs, the Ammonites and the men of Ashdod heard that the repairs to Jerusalem's walls had gone ahead and that the gaps were being closed, they were very angry. They all plotted together to come and fight against Jerusalem and stir up trouble against it. But we prayed to our God and posted a guard day and night to meet this threat.*
>
> Nehemiah 4:6–9

Nehemiah's strategy for the defense of Jerusalem included posting a guard who would keep a watchful eye out for enemies. This is an extremely wise move for the ongoing protection of your marriage as well. For the purposes of this chapter, let's define a *guard* as; *a person who watches out for the overall welfare of your marriage.* As mentioned in the last chapter, we recommend that you and your spouse have someone in your lives who will regularly provide you with wise counsel and hold you accountable to the standards in your marriage. We both have prayer/accountability partners who stand guard and keep watch over our relationship. We've given these individuals full permission to ask us tough questions, check-up on the progress of our marriage, and hold us accountable to our commitments.

I (Clint) prayed for months before God led me to my first prayer partner. Had the choice been mine, I'm sure I would not have selected the man He chose for me. After getting to know Johnathan, however, I could see that God designed a perfect fit for both of us. We are very different in our hobbies and interests, but following the Lord and nurturing our relationships with our wives remains at the core of our hearts. Over the years that we've been prayer partners, we've gone through a lot together. To this day, Johnathan and I still ask each other tough questions regarding our spiritual growth, marriages, business dealings, and areas of ministry.

The importance of maintaining a strong defense and ongoing support system for your marriage is something we teach couples in our workshops and seminars. Unfortunately, many people will drop their means of support and accountability once the worst of the disaster has passed. That's a blatant error. Having an accountability/prayer partner should be an agreement you maintain throughout *every* season of your marriage.

We've developed a checklist for helping you find an accountability/prayer partner.

Qualities of an Accountability/Prayer Partner

— A mature, married Christian of the same gender. (It is *never* appropriate to have an accountability partner of the opposite sex.)
— A person who seeks God's will daily, through prayer and the Word.
— A person with whom you can be honest and vulnerable.
— A person who can ask you difficult questions.
— A person who is faithful and reliable.
— A person who is an advocate for your marriage.
— A person who will pray for you regularly.
— A person who will maintain confidentiality.
— A person who is willing to listen without judging.

Of course, locating the right person begins and ends with prayer because God already has him/her in mind for you. If you don't have an accountability/prayer partner, begin praying for one.

Once again we must restate that even as things improve and your restoration continues, don't drop your accountability/prayer partner. This person will serve as an integral part of maintaining your focus on God first, and then on your spouse. He/she will provide you with perspective when you're selfish, wisdom when you're uncertain, hope when you're discouraged, and accountability when you're tempted.

Developing a Weekly Strategy

Nehemiah was fully aware of the importance in securing Jerusalem's gates against future attacks. No sooner was their reconstruction complete, than did Nehemiah mobilize forces to deploy a system for their ongoing defense (Nehemiah 7:1–3). Some research even indicates that in order to fireproof the gates, they were dipped and coated in bronze.

Part of our ongoing proactive strategy for protecting our marriage actually started six months before we remarried. Living on opposite coasts at the time, we asked God for a way to protect what He was doing in our relationship. As a result, every Sunday evening by phone, we took turns reading Scripture and discussing its application to our lives. We also shared prayer requests for the week ahead and closed our conversations by praying together. One week Penny would lead our devotional time and the next week, it was my turn.

To this day, the habit of weekly devotions continues to be one of the foundational proactive strategies of protecting and defending our marriage. Every Sunday night we sit together in our living room for one hour. We read a passage of the Bible together and talk about its application for our lives. This is our time to connect in a meaningful way and to make sure there aren't any problems brewing between us. During that hour we also align our calendars for the coming week so we can guard against over-committed schedules or breakdowns in communication, and prepare for what's in store for the week ahead.

If you've never had a couples' devotional time, here is a basic outline of what we suggest. All you need is a Bible, a pencil, a notebook/journal, and an open heart.

- Take turns leading the devotional time so that only one spouse is responsible for preparing each week.

- Open each session in prayer, asking God to reveal Himself to you through His Word.

- The leader should select a passage of the Bible that's been meaningful to him/her during the week. We suggest you use a relatively short passage while you're getting started. The spouse who is leading should read the passage aloud while the other person follows along in his/her own Bible.

- Relate the selected passage to your lives through discussion. The person leading may also choose to share something meaningful from his/her daily devotional that relates to the topic. The leader should explain why he/she chose this Scripture and devotional reading and how it applies to him/her.

- As you discuss God's Word, ask questions and give each other time to respond to what you've read. Don't criticize your spouse's responses, just listen. This is not a time to debate or argue opinions. Rather, it is a time to apply the Word to your lives.

- Lay out your calendars and discuss what the week ahead looks like. Put plans in place. Discuss any needs for support. Be certain you're not over-committing yourselves.

- Take turns sharing prayer requests and then, pray together for the coming week. It's best if both spouses write down the requests in separate notebooks/journals. Be certain to share praises from the prior week as well. You'll be amazed at all the answers to prayer from week-to-week as you continue meeting. A notebook/journal is a great way to trace what transpires.

You may not necessarily call what the Israelites did as having a devotional time. But, after they'd completed the rebuilding of Jerusalem's walls and settled in their towns, Nehemiah assembled them and the Word of God was read in their midst. Nehemiah 8:8 says, *"They read from the Book of the Law of God, making it clear and giving the meaning so that the people could understand what was being read."*

The people responded to the Word by confessing their sins and praying for forgiveness. They reflected on the evil things they had done (as well as those of their forefathers) and recalled God's deliverance (Nehemiah 9). In addition, they made a binding agreement to keep a covenant of obedience (Nehemiah 9:38).

Make your weekly time together a binding agreement and a top priority for the stabilization of your marriage and family. We know you're busy. We are too. Life's demands are intense these days, and that is exactly why it's so critical to create a system to keep your relationship stable. With a fortified marriage, nothing can come between you and your spouse as the pace of life quickens and demands are placed at your doorstep.

Agree to come together for one hour once a week, and decide on a regular time and place to meet. Fifty-two hours a year is a small price to pay for something as priceless as your marriage. We suggest you meet on the same day and time each week so this devotional becomes a part of your normal routine. Choose a location that is quiet and free from distractions and have an "interruption plan" should a problem unexpectedly arise. (What will you do if the phone rings, a child needs tending, and so forth?) Over time, our family and friends have learned that, unless it's an emergency, our devotional time shouldn't be interrupted.

It took us a few months of practice to get a good feel for how this devotional time worked best. Give yourself a chance to get settled into a routine. There have been many times when irritations occurred between us just prior to our start time. On those evenings, the temptation to forsake meeting was immense. However, we still kept our commitment and prayed through our problems, even when it felt awkward or we didn't feel like being together. God has never been negligent in answering even the feeblest of prayers we've offered to Him in the midst of our struggles. Like us, some weeks your devotional time will seem easier than others. Eventually, however, it will become a foundational part of your marriage that you'll look forward to each week.

If you have small children in the home, we know that finding an hour together isn't easy. However, we encourage you to be persistent in praying for a way to adapt the idea of a devotional time to fit your situation. Even young children can be taught that mommy and daddy need some time alone.

Several years ago, we were sent to Italy as marriage missionaries. Our charge was to come alongside a couple who had hit a point of severe crisis in their marriage. One of the tools we taught them was how to have a weekly devotional time. With four active children in the home, finding time alone together was challenging. But, with persistence, they found a time that worked best for their marriage and family. In addition, they gathered their children for a family devotional each week and encouraged each child to take turns leading it.

We believe so passionately in the value of this tool that we wrote a year's worth of short devotionals into a book entitled, *Dance Lessons—A Weekly Devotional Guide for Couples.*[14] It follows the same format we suggest in this chapter: a passage of Scripture, a short story, application, questions to consider, and a prayer for the week. The stories and questions contained in *Dance Lessons* were carefully designed to help meet the challenges of restoring a marriage.

Being Equipped and Ready

As mentioned at the start of this chapter, five years after we remarried, we moved from California to Florida. While we were relieved to be free from the threat of earthquakes, we now faced the uncertainties of hurricanes and inclement weather common to the east coast. Because Clint had lived in Florida a few years prior to our reconciliation, he knew how important it was to properly hurricane-proof our home.

"If a hurricane hits, we need to be ready to board-up the windows," he explained. "If the windows blow out, the rest of the house won't stand against the storm."

Clint went on to explain that the windows were extremely vulnerable in high winds, yet so very vital for maintaining the structural integrity of our home. Therefore, all the windows had to be completely covered. Clint worked day and night for two straight weeks, drilling metal studs into the stucco around each window of our home. Then, he cut, fit, and labeled the various pieces of plywood so they could be quickly affixed over each window and bolted into place should a storm arise.

His work to hurricane-proof our house created quite a stir in the neighborhood. Nerves were rattled and rumors circulated as to why Clint was working so hard to prepare for something that might never happen. Many people stopped to question his craftsmanship and to find out if he had some kind of inside scoop as to the arrival of a hurricane. After one day when numerous neighbors had stopped by, Clint came into the house and said, "Now I know how Noah must have felt!"

I laughed and replied, "Yeah, and now I know how Noah's *wife* must have felt."

One man who came by said something that both of us thought was so very typical of what people do in their marriages today, "I'm not doing anything to my house right now. I'll just deal with it if a hurricane hits."

Like the neighbors who think we're a bit neurotic to go to such extreme measures to hurricane-proof our home, many people don't truly understand the precautions that must be taken to protect and stabilize your marriage. Expect some odd reactions from people. We've met many folks who don't understand the great emphasis we continue to place on mending our marriage and the lengths to which we'll go to ensure it remains well-protected. We've come to realize, however, that unless you've lost something precious, you don't really understand what it means to have a second chance. We remember, all too well, what was like to lose our marriage and the eleven years that we can never get back.

Nehemiah also knew better than to take the security of Jerusalem for granted or to get lax and let down his guard. He knew the exact places where vulnerability still existed. He knew what do to protect the city and took the appropriate precautions to ensure its safety. At times, his protective measures may have seemed extreme to onlookers as well.

> *Those who carried materials did their work with one hand and held a weapon in the other.*
>
> Nehemiah 4:17

> *Neither I nor my brothers nor my men nor the guards with me took off our clothes; each had his weapon, even when he went for water.*
>
> Nehemiah 4:23

Not only did Nehemiah equip and arm the workers along the wall, they also labored long and hard; well past their usual quitting time. Nehemiah's tenacity and the protective measures carried out by the Jews are just two of the many applications we can examine and apply.

Take a moment to visualize those two verses in relation to your marriage. Picture yourselves with a tool in one hand and a weapon in the other. Commentator J. Vernon McGee explains that the tool (most likely a trowel) represents that believers must build themselves up in their faith. The trowel is symbolic of the inner work we must allow God to do in our hearts at all times. The weapon (most likely a sword) represents the sword of the Spirit which is the Word.[15] We must wield God's Word as the sword that will never fail to protect and defend our marriage.

Nehemiah never dealt with his enemies in his own strength and neither should you. For as many assaults as were launched at him, Nehemiah continued the work and faithfully called on God to take action on his behalf. He never wasted his energy to launch a counter-assault. Not only must you continually rely on God to defend your marriage, but also realize that you don't have to do it alone. God is raising up restored couples and ministries to take back the territory of marriage and family all across our nation and abroad. Organizations such as the *Association of Marriage and Family Ministries (AMFM)* have united a mega-network of grassroots ministries whose sole purpose is to equip the local church with resources to fortify marriages and families. AMFM realizes, as have we, that when a marriage is healthy, the family will be healthy. When the family is healthy, the church will be healthy. And a healthy church can change the world!

Spend time researching some of the books and websites listed at the end of *Marriage on the Mend*. The ministries represented have excellent resources to assist you in restoring and strengthening your marriage and family. Many of these organizations even specialize in particular areas of healing and recovery from issues such as infidelity or sexual addiction.

Additionally, as stated in a previous chapter, become a student of marriage. Make it a point to arm yourselves with useful strategies and tips such as those offered at marriage conferences, workshops, and retreats. Ask other couples for their recommendations and commit to attending at least one seminar, retreat, or marriage conference each year.

Another simple strategy to strengthen your marriage is to interact with new people. About a year after we remarried, we joined a small group of couples at our church and gathered with them for weekly prayer, study, and fellowship. Through our times together, we were able to exchange advice, books, resources, and ideas to help shore up the foundation of our marriages. We also knew that because the bond between us became strong, we could call on one another in times of crisis. It was through this group that we found our prayer partners as well.

Keep at It

Take notice of Nehemiah's perseverance. As trouble came to him in waves, he still persevered and made progress. Also notice that the assaults his enemies attempted were progressive in nature. When one tactic didn't work, they launched a more comprehensive one to interfere with the rebuilding. At one point, Nehemiah's opponents were so desperate, they tried to intimidate him with false accusations that threatened to malign his reputation (Nehemiah 6:1–14). His response to their threats was a technique we should all retain in our hearts and minds and be swift to employ when the intensity of the battle heats up.

Sanballat and Geshem sent me this message: "Come, let us meet together in one of the villages on the plain of Ono." But they were scheming to harm me; so I sent

> *messengers to them with this reply: "I am carrying on a*
> *great project and cannot go down. Why should I stop*
> *work while I leave it and go down to you?" Four times*
> *they sent me the same message, and each time I gave*
> *them the same answer.*
>
> Nehemiah 6:2–4

Despite repeated attempts to trap, intimidate and distract him with lies and unfounded accusations, Nehemiah employed a sort of *broken record technique*. He prayed and prayed…and prayed again. Four times his enemies sent a message and four times he met their message with the same answer. If you read further in Nehemiah 6, you'll discover that these troublemakers continued to pester Nehemiah, but he held fast to his convictions, prayed, and kept on working.

Even with all the forms of opposition and oppression his enemies threw in his direction, progress was made on the restoration of Jerusalem because Nehemiah had a variety of reactive *and* proactive tools and strategies that were deployed at each sign of trouble. We pray that, at this stage of your journey, the same can also be said for your marriage. In the next chapter, we'll help you understand the importance of assessing the progress of your marriage with God's measuring stick in order to continue moving forward in the healing process.

> *Then I said to the nobles, the officials and the rest of*
> *the people, "The work is extensive and spread out, and*
> *we are widely separated from each other along the*
> *wall. Wherever you hear the trumpet, join us there. Our*
> *God will fight for us!"*
>
> Nehemiah 4:19–20

CHAPTER EXERCISES

Prayer for a Stable Marriage

God, as we face our problems together, show us how to create a strategy that strengthens and defends our marriage against *any* form of internal or external opposition. Give us the strength to rise against the real Enemy and the wisdom to unite as one flesh. Even more than having You change our circumstances, it's our desire to have You change our hearts. We ask You for a stable and resilient marriage and we commit to never looking for a way out of our relationship, come what may. Give us Your effective battle plan and grant us the strength to work together; facing every trial as a team. When You want us to be still because You will fight for us, help us hear and heed Your advice. Provide us with resources, accountability and wise counsel so that *every* aspect of our marriage is protected and pleasing to You. In Jesus' name. Amen.

Making Connections

If you don't have an accountability/prayer partner, pray about finding one. Ask God to lead you to the right person. Take a few moments to write down some of the qualities, common interests, and personality traits you hope this person will have, but be willing for God to surprise you. Be sure to review the checklist for choosing an accountability/prayer partner on page 214.

Scripture Reading

Read Nehemiah 8 before answering the questions.

Questions to Consider

1. Think of at least one example of an internal conflict and one example of an external conflict you're presently facing. Which conflict is more difficult for you to deal with? Why?

2. Of all the tools mentioned in this chapter, what one or two ideas can you immediately apply to your circumstances?

3. When do you find it most difficult to persevere in the restoration process?

4. What are the positive changes your spouse has made over the past several weeks, despite opposition? Verbally affirm the changes you've noticed.

5. In Chapter 8, Nehemiah assembled the people together in one place. What was the purpose of this assembly? What do you notice about the response and emotions of the people?

6. Look over your marriage timeline again. Can you identify the places where accountability/prayer partners would have helped to provide you with wise counsel regarding big decisions and life events? As you look at the blank section of the timeline (which represents what is to come) discuss the ways you will use some of the proactive strategies from this chapter to approach the future.

Eight years into our marriage, we bottomed out. We had two children under the age of three and Steve was working out-of-town a lot—sometimes only returning home every other weekend. Not only were we facing these challenges, but we'd over-committed ourselves by leading Bible studies, teaching Sunday school, and being regularly involved in more social activities than we could manage. On the outside, we looked like the perfect Christian couple, but on the inside, the busyness and sinfulness of life was more than our young marriage could handle.

Time pressures, emotional distance, and selfishness were driving us into real trouble and before long there was more bad than good in our marriage. We loved each other and really didn't want a divorce, but we were without hope that things could really change.

Through some loving mentors who wanted to help us, we realized we couldn't make our marriage work without the power of God's love in it. Seeking God, rather than wallowing in our circumstances, was the key to making some lasting changes. Our mentors gave us hope. They assured us that God was big enough for the task and we were to look to Him, not each other. They had us rewrite our marriage vows and commitments, along with other practical things. For example, we had to promise to put the kids down at a consistent time each night and to use that time to talk.

Continued on the next page…

Continued from the previous page…

We've now been married over forty years, most of them great. However, our marriage is not simply an accomplishment. It's a process that takes effort every day…forever. From time to time, we still have to regroup because the demands of life threaten to crowd in on us. We've finally learned that busyness is not from God, but it's so easy to get caught up in its trap. Thankfully, we now have several strategies to keep our focus on God and to be intentional about time together. We pray and talk together every day—out loud and eye-to-eye. Actually, we talk "feet-to-feet" from both ends of the couch. We call this, "talk time," and it is something that can be requested by either of us. When a request is made, we set a time and meet on the couch. In addition, we're both willing to wave the flag that says we need time together and we have several phrases that signal distress such as, "I need some of your time," or, "My bucket is empty."

A healthy marriage requires discipline and commitment, but with those things comes great rewards in closeness. However you do it, marriage is all about intentionally making quality time to focus together on your relationship. And, never mind the excuses. Just do it!

Steve and Shay Freeman
AMFM Marriage Ambassadors
Little Rock, Arkansas

Chapter 11 – Managing Your Margins

When we were married the first time, we had little understanding of how important it was to regularly and accurately assess the progress of our relationship. We'd always been goal-oriented students and professionals, but it never dawned on either of us that we should have goals in our marriage, nor did we realize that we should take time out to sit down and talk about our relationship.

Before returning to California to remarry Penny, I had the opportunity to attend a seminar where the speaker shared that he regularly escaped with his wife to discuss how things were going in their marriage and family. During the course of the seminar, he also discussed the ways they set goals together in various areas of their relationship in order to make sure it was consistently growing. I was so intrigued by what was said that I told Penny all about it and asked her if she'd be open to implementing something like this into our remarriage. We were doing some of this work during our weekly devotional time, but that really didn't allow us to stop long enough and take a step back to gain a broader perspective.

Over time, our discussions about all of this gave birth to what we now call a *Mini-Marriage Retreat*. This chapter focuses on the basic explanation of how a Mini-Marriage Retreat works and provides you with some helpful "how-to" tips to implement this idea into your marriage.

In order to continue growing, changing, and moving forward, you need to be able to set and assess goals, discuss feelings, communicate struggles, and share dreams; all without the interruptions and busyness common amidst everyday life. People set short and long-range goals to grow their businesses. Why not take the same approach to growing your marriage?

It's our hope that by the end of this chapter, you'll come to understand the inherent value of a Mini-Marriage Retreat and agree to make these a priority. In order to accurately assess the progression of your restoration, you'll need two important things: time and tools. You must ask God to help you make the time, but all the tools you'll need are included in this chapter.

What are *Marriage Margins*?

Chronic busyness is something we see plaguing most marriages and families today. There's no room in people's daily schedules to allow for reflection, solitude, assessment, prayer, quality conversation, and other things that require stillness and focused attention. Instead, these crucial elements of nurturing relationships are devalued and dominated by an endless stream of activities.

Most families spend their days running from one place to another at a frenzied pace. Technology and mass media seem to feed an insatiable thirst for this kind of busyness. While we know that tight schedules are somewhat inherent in this day and age, we also sense that a growing number of people possess a compulsion for an activity-based existence. At one point in our lives, so did we. However, we now see that the overly-hectic lifestyle that characterized our first marriage eventually contributed to its demise.

We boldly caution you that over-booking your lives will make your marriage and family a much easier target for division. In contrast, learning to place adequate and appropriate *margins* around your marriage (time and space intentionally set aside to assess growth) will dramatically contribute to the health and well-being of your lives together.

Building margins into your marriage means that you give yourself permission to take full advantage of opportunities to check-out from the obligations and responsibilities of everyday living and to check-in with each other in the areas of life that matter most. Think of this intentional space around your marriage in the same way that margins must surround a page of text. Margins exist to create and enhance a sense of order on a page so that meaning can be conveyed. Margins of time and space set around your marriage do the same thing.

Several times throughout the book of Nehemiah, we see that this faithful leader knew the value of stopping everything in order to pull God's people together. His reasons for doing so included garnering additional strength, engaging in corporate prayer, assessing progress, making changes, dealing with problems, taking oaths, forming alliances, creating covenants, fasting, confession, worship, and the reading of God's Word (see Nehemiah 5:7, 12; 7:5; Chapters 8–13). Nehemiah knew that maintaining reconciled relationships and focusing on what really mattered was (and still is) extraordinarily close to God's heart.

Putting margins around your relationship will involve a deliberate, unwavering commitment to not allow the tyranny of the urgent to keep you from taking stock of your surroundings and making necessary changes on a regular basis. Look at it this way: you can't change a tire or get a tune-up unless you pull off the side of the road and stop the car.

How God Measures Marriage

Mini-Marriage Retreats are all about assessing the growth (or lack thereof) in your relationship. But, before we explain more about how these retreats work, it's essential to understand some truths about measuring your marriage the way that God does.

By now, you know that men and women have drastically different wiring. Given this fact, without God's perspective and measuring stick, it's virtually impossible to accurately assess your marriage or agree on what it will take to keep it moving forward.

For example, as mentioned in an earlier chapter, I (Clint) am very linear. Processes, models, and structures are innate parts of how I function day-to-day. Many men have these same tendencies. For the most part, my ways of functioning in life are very contrary to Penny's. Creativity and thinking outside-the-box help her view, process, and respond to life. These differences, along with many others, make our marriage both an exciting adventure and a real challenge. In our first marriage, we didn't understand that the different ways we were created should drive us to follow hard after God's ways. Instead, we worked against each other to get and make our own ways. Now, we realize that allowing Him to use our different temperaments to balance each other out draws us closer together. The result is that we become a compliment to each other instead of a stumbling block.

Like us, your personalities, genders, ages, backgrounds, qualities, and quirks can skew your perspective on just about everything, including your marriage. Therefore, you'll need to seek God's vision and perspective in assessing your relationship, rather than relying on your own. Basically, the only way to be accurate in your viewpoints and opinions is to measure your marriage the way God does. There are three vital truths to understanding the ways God measures a marriage that we'll explain briefly before continuing.

Turn on your TV and you will quickly see the way the world measures a successful marriage: making money, raising smart kids, acquiring possessions, and having great sex. But, throughout the Bible, there is evidence that *God's measuring stick is always inverted* in comparison to that of the world. This truth is best demonstrated by Jesus who made such radical statements as, *"Blessed are the meek, for they will inherit the earth"* (Matthew 5:5). *"Whoever finds his life will lose it, and whoever loses his life for my sake will find it"* (Matthew 10:39). *"For he who is least among you all—he is the greatest."* (Luke 9:48).

For years, we've searched Christ's teachings in the New Testament, as well as the writings of His apostles. Frankly, we've lost count of the infinite number of examples of this *inverted* sort of thinking. We now refer to this truth as God's *Law of Inversion*. It's from this very principle that we derived the name for our non-profit organization, *Inverse Ministries.* Living contrary to how the world defines success, accomplishment, marriage, ministry, and so forth, is what we strive for everyday. It's an upstream swim, but we're committed to measuring every aspect of our lives the way God does.

The second truth you must understand regarding the way God measures marriage is that, for Him, *the bigger picture is always in full view.* We see, in part, what He sees in whole. The best passage from the Bible that exemplifies this truth is found in Isaiah 55:8–9. *"For my thoughts are not your thoughts, neither are your ways my ways,"* declares the LORD. *"As the heavens are higher than the earth, so are my ways higher than your ways and my thoughts than your thoughts."* This passage is the plumb line we hold to in every area of our lives.

How would a shift in perspective change your marriage right now? In what ways has your perspective left you short-sighted? Regularly praying that God would expand your perspective on life and relationships would be a very wise move. As human beings, the capacity to consider much more than our own viewpoint is severely limited, but the Holy Spirit can certainly broaden our scope.

Finally, the third truth you must remember regarding the way God measures a marriage is that *the eternal perspective is always His top priority.* One biblical example that backs up this truth is the account of Jesus and a rich young man (Matthew 19:16–24). When a wealthy fellow asks Jesus to tell him what's lacking in his life and His relationship with God, Jesus responds with a very unpopular answer. *"If you want be perfect, go, sell your possessions and give to the poor, and you will have treasure in heaven. Then come, follow me"* (Matthew 19:21). If you're familiar with this story then you know that instead of following Jesus, the young man turned and walked away. You can almost hear him muttering underneath his breath and sulking, "If that's what it takes to follow You, I'll pass."

If Jesus came back to earth today, would the priorities in your marriage and family be in *complete* alignment with God's eternal priorities? In what ways are you and your spouse seeking God's kingdom in heaven as a priority over your comfort on earth? These questions merit some sober consideration.

Once you begin to grasp the wisdom behind these three truths regarding how God measures marriage and apply them to your lives, your perception will be transformed and united under Him. There are few things more powerful than humbly submitting your differences, temperaments, strengths, innate qualities, and quirks under the authority of God and the power of the Holy Spirit. As this happens, you're wholly joined together in the spiritually intimate way God designed your marriage to function.

Getting Away with God

Having explained the ways in which God measures marriage, we'll now move into a comprehensive explanation as to how the Mini-Marriage Retreat exemplifies these truths, sets margins around your relationship, and helps you move your marriage closer toward His grand design.

The concept behind the Mini-Marriage Retreat is rather simple because, frankly, marriage is complicated enough. These retreats consist of a regular time set aside every three months for the purpose of measuring your marriage. Based on our experiences of taking over twenty-five Mini-Marriage Retreats as of this writing, we attest to the fact that this simple structure has single-handedly altered the course of our lives more than either one of us ever expected.

Once each quarter, we set aside everything except God and our marriage. E-mails and to-do lists are left behind and cell phones are turned off. Now, you may be thinking that getting away with your spouse once during a year would be a financial or logistical challenge, let alone three or four times. But, please don't dismiss this concept without reading the whole chapter, praying together, and allowing God to modify these retreats to fit your marriage, family, jobs, schedules, and budget. Engaging in our little getaways isn't easy for us either. However, we know the agony of losing our marriage. Perhaps you do, too. Had we instituted an idea like this the first time around, we may never have gone our separate ways.

Mini-Marriage Retreats are scheduled onto our calendars as a priority at the start of every year. What works best for our marriage and ministry is to get away in February, May, August, and November. While we understand that you may not be able to take a Mini-Marriage Retreat once each quarter, we recommend at least twice a year as a starting point.

About three weeks before a retreat, we begin praying about the specific location God wants us to go. What helps alleviate additional stress is selecting a destination not far from home. In fact, we've been known to check into an inexpensive hotel only ten minutes away from where we live. Over the years, we've kept a record of hotels that are in close proximity to our home, accommodating to guests, and inexpensive. We usually rotate around to those hotels, unless God lets us know that He has something else in mind. As missionaries, our budget is very limited. So, to save money, we use hotels that serve a continental breakfast as part of the room package. The point is not *where we go* on these retreats, but *what we do together* during the days we're away.

If you have small children at home and/or cannot afford to get away, there are options. One suggestion is that you pair up with another couple in the same boat. When it's time for your Mini-Marriage Retreat, they watch your children. When it's time for their retreat, you do the same for them. Another idea is to swap houses, condos, or apartments with a couple or family you trust. Perhaps the couple you partner with can watch your children (and theirs) in your home and you can use a guest room in their home as your retreat location (and vice-versa). The point is that you are completely alone and not in your own house so as to avoid distractions. Discussing this idea with another interested couple may also lend itself to other creative solutions to solve childcare issues and budget shortfalls.

What a Mini-Marriage Retreat Looks Like

Typically, we leave in the late afternoon of our first day. After checking into our hotel, we freshen up and go out on a simple date. We alternate planning these date nights so each of us has a chance to decide what we'll do and where we'll go. During dinner, we talk over some of our expectations for our time away. Our night out is to be a time of enjoying each other's company without the stress of schedules, ministry, commitments, and/or problems.

The next morning after breakfast and our individual quiet times, we take a long walk. Then, with our Bibles, journals, and the list of goals from our last Mini-Marriage Retreat in hand, we find a quiet place to work, such as the hotel pool area. In the warmer months, we can usually locate a nearby park or picnic table. When it's too cold to be outside, we find a quiet conference room in the hotel or just stay in our room. The hotel registrar is usually very helpful in assisting us with what's in the area.

Once we find a place to settle, we begin our discussion with prayer, asking God to guide us. We open our journals and begin reviewing the goals that were set during our previous Mini-Marriage Retreat (three months earlier). Reviewing our past goals usually takes about ninety minutes. (Obviously, when you take your very first Mini-Marriage Retreat, you won't have a previous list of goals to look over.)

While we're reviewing our goals from the prior three months, we look at the things God helped us accomplish and discuss whether or not the goals that weren't reached were a result of our own neglect, or because He led us in different direction. The answer to that question determines whether or not the unmet goals are carried over into the next quarter, or not.

Regardless of the results, this time of reviewing and reflecting causes us to give thanks to God for helping us work toward reaching our marriage goals. Reviewing these goals also provides us with a wonderful opportunity to complement each other about the growth we've seen in particular areas. Over time, we've realized that the processes God uses to help us reach our goals are often far more important than the achievements themselves. In order to maintain God's perspective on your marriage, you must always give ample consideration to the means, as well as the end.

Husbands, I want to stop right here and speak directly to you—man-to-man. Like me, you may not be as relationally-gifted as is your wife. For some of you, just the thought of talking in-depth for twenty minutes is a real stretch. Give it time. When we first started doing this, the entire review and planning time lasted about thirty minutes and I was done. Penny wanted to discuss and develop our marriage standards and I couldn't even go there.

Wives, please give your husbands a chance to ease into this process. Trust me when I tell you that your conversations together will become more fluid and natural. In time, you'll be so amazed at the things God does in your marriage through these retreats that you'll look forward to each one.

Once we've reviewed our goals from the prior quarter, we break for lunch before setting goals for the next three months. Following lunch, we spend several hours discussing and setting our new goals for the quarter to come. Remember, we've taken many of these retreats and our dialogue has expanded and deepened over time. Again, allow us to use our first retreat as an example.

Our goals back then consisted of committing to the date for our next retreat and setting four or five very simple goals. Keeping things simple at the start ensured our success and built up our confidence. Since then, our Mini-Marriage Retreats have enriched our relationship so much that we often lose track of time and have to be careful not to set too many goals. Mini-Marriage Retreats have been so valuable that about a year after we formed *Inverse Ministries*, we started using the same quarterly goal-setting system to measure our ministry and move it forward.

Once we finish determining our goals for the coming quarter, they're offered to God in prayer; always giving Him the permission to change, rearrange, remove, or replace what we've written down. Before we conclude our planning time, we also ask God for His clarity and direction regarding a date and location for our next Mini-Marriage Retreat.

Because day two's conversation is quite involved, we plan an evening that doesn't require a lot of deep thought or discussion such as going to a movie, or hanging out in a local bookstore or café.

The next morning, we pack up to head home. Since the hotel check-out time is usually around 11:00am, there's just enough time to meet with God, pack up our things, and grab some breakfast. We pray that as we return home, God will help us transition back to our individual routines and responsibilities as well as carry out the things He's planned for us. Again, having only a short drive home saves time as we make the transition back into our regular schedules.

The Seven Focus Areas

There are seven focus areas for the Mini-Marriage Retreat. Granted, you may decide to make modifications to better fit your marriage and family. We've discovered, however, that these seven areas seem to cover the basic functioning of most marriages.

- **Spiritual**–This is the first category of the Mini-Marriage Retreat because it is the most important. Goals in this area include anything related to your spiritual growth and development individually and as a couple.

- **Relationships**–This area includes your relationship and communication with each another, your children, extended family members, prayer partners, and friends.

- **Health/Fitness**–Goals in this category include getting regular exercise, monitoring your weight, making medical appointments, or anything else that keeps your body in good shape.

- **Professional**–Goals that focus on your career and/or pursuits in education belong in this category.

- **Financial**–This area includes your tithes and offerings, upcoming expenses, savings plans, taxes, and other financial matters.

240

- **Home**–Repairs, furnishings, or renovations are discussed under this category.

- **Big Dreams and Possibilities**–This area includes your individual and joint hopes and dreams.

Sample of Penny's Mini-Marriage Journal Page

Spiritual Goals:

   Penny's spiritual goals-
   ✓ Memorize my life passage Isaiah 61:1–4
       Read two books on fasting
   ✓ Increase prayer time on Mondays and Fridays

   Clint's spiritual goals-
   ✓ Begin new study on life of Christ
   ✓ Design disciples' cross retreat for men
   ✓ Continue focus on journaling as intercession

   Spiritual goals for our marriage-
   ✓ Continue Sunday night devotionals
       Find new home church in Florida
   ✓ Read one book together – Clint's turn to pick

Organize your Mini-Marriage Retreat journal or notes in a way that works best for you. As you can see, I (Penny) divide my pages into the various focus areas and keep track of our individual goals, as well as the goals for our marriage. The goals we agree upon in each area are listed accordingly. I like to use check marks to keep track of whether or not goals are accomplished.

There are several important aspects to each of the focus areas that we'll clarify in the following pages so you have a greater understanding as to the kinds of things discussed in each category. Our ideas aren't meant to be exhaustive by any means. Again, you and your spouse may want to expand on these areas or even include additional ideas. We can't stress enough that you must adapt the focus areas and the particular items discussed to best fit your marriage and family and not the other way around. And, to ensure your success, it's important to start out slowly.

If your Mini-Marriage Retreats are going to be successful in helping you grow and heal as a couple, the categories and goals must mean something to both of you. When you set goals, keep in mind how much time will pass between the date they're set and when you'll revisit them during your next retreat. It's also a good idea to have both spouses write down the agreed-upon goals in their own separate journals or notebooks and to continue praying over them. Our goals and notes are kept in our own individual journals so we can refer to them as needed. It's been exciting to watch God work in each area over time. Those journals have become a historical and spiritual record of all that He has done in our marriage thus far.

Now that we've briefly explained the seven goal areas, let's spend some time unpacking each one in greater detail and give you some examples of goals that might fall under each category.

Spiritual Goals

As mentioned earlier, included in this category are our individual spiritual goals and our goals as a couple. For example, as an individual, I (Clint) may be feeling led to memorize some Scripture during the coming quarter or to read a book on a particular topic. Or, I may sense that God wants me to make some changes to the time I spend with Him each day. Things Penny might include as her spiritual goals might be spending more time in prayer and worship, or listening to a series of audio teachings on a book of the Bible. During one particular quarter, I wanted to focus on memorizing 1st, 2nd, and 3rd John, so I wrote those goals down and told Penny I would recite the passages I memorized to her during our next retreat.

One important aspect of this category is that when I share my spiritual goals with Penny, she listens, asks clarifying questions, and writes down my goals in her journal. I do the same when she shares her spiritual goals with me. That way, we hold each other accountable to our commitments and pray for each other's success. We're also careful not to condemn or criticize when goals aren't reached or when we set goals that are different from each other (which is often the case, given our personalities).

As a couple, goals in this category may be things like reading a book together during the coming quarter, joining a small group study, or agreeing on a time to fast. For several months we emphasized the work of the Holy Spirit in our lives and wanted to learn more about His power. So at one of our retreats, we agreed to read a book together on that topic.

A word of caution: It's important to be sure you're not substituting "doing things for God" in exchange for engaging in the spiritual disciplines that will grow you closer to Him. Overall, what we've discovered about this specific category is that it pleases God and brings Him honor. He continues to show us new ways to seek after His heart. God wants nothing more than for His children to want more of Him.

Relationship Goals

In this category, we include our marriage and other relationships that are close to us. We discuss upcoming family get-togethers, birthdays, special events, and the ways in which we will spend quality time with loved ones. Because my (Penny's) family is so large and there are many events, birthdays, etc., looking ahead and discussing these things in advance helps Clint to not feel overwhelmed.

We never want to take for granted the people that God has entrusted to us. This category helps ensure that we don't forget what matters most. For example, during the first two years of our remarriage, Clint's grandmother had failing health prior to her death at age 101. So, we agreed to travel to the assisted living center where she was staying and to visit her regularly. While we were saddened when Oma passed away, we were free of any regrets about not spending quality time with her.

Your relationships with your children belong in this category. Perhaps there is one child you need to spend more time with in the coming months, or there are strained relationships between your children and you need to oversee some changes. One goal might be to have a family meeting at least twice during the coming quarter so that issues and concerns can be openly discussed. Again, make this category fit your family, not the other way around.

Our relationships with our prayer partners and close friends are also placed in this category. Relationships we may be struggling with are discussed as well, in order to continue seeking God and communicating our concerns.

Of course, our interactions as husband and wife are of the utmost importance here. We discuss any areas of difficulty we may be having with each other and set appropriate goals so that change can occur. An example of a goal in this area might be to schedule a date night once a week, or to be more intentional with each other regarding affection.

Openly talking about sexual intimacy also falls under this category. We never discussed sexual intimacy or physical needs when we were married the first time, but we do now. Of course, this isn't the only time we talk about sex, pleasure, or physical and emotional needs, but we have found that talking about these things outside of our bedroom really allows us to ask specific and thought-provoking questions and to listen to what we need from each other. For us, it would be a bit much to set goals as to how many times a week we're going to have sex, but if that's something you need to do because you're schedules aren't in sync, by all means, go for it!

The key is that you are openly and honestly discussing physical and emotional intimacy. This area is one of the greatest challenges in marriage because our differences as men and women tend to come into play here more than in other areas. Most men seek physical intimacy as a way to connect with their spouses, especially after a conflict. But, women want emotional intimacy before they'll engage in the physical. I explain this difference to couples in our seminars by telling them that most wives would put it to their husbands this way: "Honey, you're going to have to touch my heart, before you can touch my parts."

Through our work with couples, we've discovered that the stark contrast in the ways men and women are wired in this particular area is one of the main reasons infidelity is on the rise. That was certainly the case for us the first time around.

Whether or not intimacy was violated during your marriage crisis, we encourage you to prayerfully approach goal-setting and deeper discussions about these things. God longs for a marriage to be intimate in *every* way. Because God is the only one who can meet all your needs and those of your spouse, He can help you figure out what to change so that both of you feel as though your needs are being met, despite your differences.

Health/Fitness Goals

Anything related to keeping your body in good working condition is placed in this category. The Bible says that our body is God's dwelling place and a temple of the Holy Spirit (1 Corinthians 3:16; 6:19; 2 Corinthians 6:16). Therefore, it's essential to take good care of ourselves so that we can serve God well while we're on this side of heaven.

As we age, we're becoming increasingly aware of how important it is to ask for God's help to remain healthy and active. Perhaps one or both of us wants to lose weight or increase our exercise during the coming quarter. Those goals would be placed in this category. Or, there may be upcoming medical or dental appointments that need to be scheduled. Deciding on the various appointments and who will be responsible for making them is also discussed. Talking about these things helps us to not put off routine appointments and exams.

We also discuss dietary concerns and the ways in which we sense God may be prompting us to make changes. For example, after experiencing some uncomfortable physical symptoms, medical exams, and blood tests, we discovered that Clint needed to make dietary changes for the health of his heart. We talked at length about how we might approach this. As a result, we decided how to make changes to our eating habits as a team, even though the goal was really Clint's.

Just as in the other categories, some of our goals under health/fitness are individual and some are made as a couple. The key is listening, supporting each other, and functioning as partners so that we can work toward each other's successes, as well as our own.

Professional Goals

Any goals or ambitions related to your career and/or education are placed in this focus area. For example, there may be classes you want to take in order to move toward your professional aspirations. When Clint moved back to California from Florida, he had to complete a series of classes to renew his teaching credential. He set a goal to take one class each quarter so he wouldn't procrastinate in getting his credential cleared or have to take all the classes at once.

Other goals in this area might include putting a personal resumé together, investigating an opportunity for a promotion or searching out a change in employment. Perhaps you know you'll be traveling for your job during the coming quarter. We see many marriages falling by the wayside because demanding travel/business schedules are out of control, swallowing too much time away from the family. Discussing upcoming trips, projects, timelines, and stressful seasons at your workplace can be very helpful, especially when there are young children in need of care and parenting. This category also helps maintain a balance between home and career.

Although we don't have small children, we must pause here and speak specifically to an issue of epidemic proportion. Countless couples are divorcing who have small children in the home. We do not mean to over-generalize here, but a high percentage of the people who contact us commonly report that the husband feels he is pulling all the weight of providing for his family and the wife feels her husband has no clue as to the demands she is facing with the children. At the end of the work day, he's exhausted and wants to be taken care of or to just zone-out for a while. His wife, however, is also exhausted from taking care of the kids all day. When her husband gets home from work, she's ready to have him take over caring for the children, or she wants to spend some time together as a family. If both parents are working outside the home (as many are today) this expands the problem to an ever greater proportion because both spouses are exhausted.

First of all, we want to make a statement of support for any stay-at-home moms and dads. Having been in public education for a combined total of over twenty years, we consider what you're doing to stay home with your kids as a necessary full-time profession—one deserving the same kind of respect and attentiveness given to careers outside the home. We encourage goals to be set under the area of career for any parents who are working in the home to raise their kids.

In an effort to walk a mile in each other's shoes, some good friends of ours recently traded places with each other. Annie is now teaching high school and her husband, Rob, is working from home, taking care of their son, and managing things around the house.

"As Rob and I have traded places," Annie said, "we're now experiencing the *exact* same feelings the other one had and it's really opened our eyes. It absolutely drives me nuts to come home and find the house a mess and Rob 'just sitting' in a chair, and it drives him crazy when I have no idea how often he has washed yet another pile of dirty dishes or picked up Nate's belongings for the umpteenth time."

Having both parents working outside the home and raising children is a difficult season. We want to remind you that this season will pass. Eventually, the kids will be out of the house. But, when that time finally comes, what will the condition of your marriage be?

The intent in bringing this common marriage scenario onto the radar screen here is not so much to solve it, but to note that if you're in this season right now, you must begin regularly discussing your feelings and compassionately listening to those of your spouse. If necessary, go through a day in each other's shoes.

Don't set your marriage on the back burner. Instead, ask for help. Many others have walked this road before you. Tap into their wisdom. Most importantly, ask God for some possible and practical options before the divide between you is so great that neither of you has the desire or the energy to cross it.

Financial Goals

Any goals related to generosity, upcoming expenses, erasing debts, savings plans, investments, or operating budgets fall into this category. If you need to get your taxes done in the coming quarter, write it down and decide what needs to happen in order to prepare for the appointment. Perhaps you know that your property taxes will be due before your next retreat and it's a huge expense. All of these things fit into this category.

As we entered our remarriage, we made several goals that, unbeknownst to either of us at the time, served to change our financial state more than anything else we'd ever done. Because the economy is taking its toll on many couples today, please allow us to unpack a few important goals that, to this day, we regularly agree upon. Once we realized that drastic positive changes were happening as a result of these practices, we agreed to recommit to them each quarter.

The first goal we commit to is that we'll tithe at least ten percent of our income. No matter what the state of our finances may appear to be, this commitment is non-negotiable. We guarantee that if you look at tithing as an option, you'll inconsistently tithe. Sometimes, we test our comfort zones and our faith by giving additional offerings over and above our tithe. Whatever we give, God out-gives us every time.

The second goal we recommit to is that if purchases are made on a credit card, they have to be paid off within the same month. Our commitment is to remain debt-free. We also pray for the overall protection of everything God has entrusted to us and ask Him to protect our health, home, appliances, and vehicle from major or unexpected expenses.

Finally, to limit any impulsive spending or temptations to live beyond our means, we agree to what we call the *one hundred dollar rule.* The way this works is that if there is any single item we'd like to purchase that costs over one hundred dollars, it must be brought to the table and discussed at our next Mini-Marriage Retreat. Gone are the days when we'd see some fancy electronic gadget or piece of furniture and purchase it on the spot. It took some getting used to, but in time, this agreement worked wonders for our financial well-being. It has eliminated spontaneous buys that we can't afford and cut out disagreements over "surprise" purchases which often contribute to conflict between many spouses. Stopping impulse buys also helped us pay off past debts and gain greater financial freedom. In addition, we discovered that getting on the same page regarding upcoming expenses helps us not be caught off guard when those bills are due.

Of course, there have been times an unexpected emergency has arisen that cost over one hundred dollars. Obviously, some expenses can't wait to be discussed at a retreat. However, what we have discovered by utilizing the one hundred dollar rule is that, overall, it helps us spend a lot less money.

When we do decide to make a large purchase (after praying about it) we always ask God to provide coupons, savings, or sales. And, after we buy something, we both place our hands on the item and ask God to bless and protect it so that it can be used for years to come.

We'll never forget the day we went out to buy some outdoor furniture for our screened-in porch. Because we knew that the table and chairs we wanted would cost more than one hundred dollars, we discussed the purchase at one of our retreats and agreed upon a reasonable budget. As is always our practice, we asked God for a good deal and within a few weeks, we found the furniture on sale at a local retailer. In addition, a five-dollar savings coupon came in the mail.

Once we arrived at the store and priced everything out, however, the total was just slightly above the amount we'd budgeted. We talked about it for a few minutes and decided to move ahead with the purchase. Then, while we were standing at the cash register, an elderly gentleman walked up to us and asked, "Can you use this?" Imagine our astonishment when he handed us a coupon for a twenty percent discount! He hadn't heard any of our discussion, but was just passing some savings along. We have dozens of stories (enough to merit an entire chapter) just like that one.

Modifying these tips to fit your marriage will make a drastic impact on your financial health. Perhaps your rule needs to be reduced to fifty dollars or increased to some amount other than one hundred. Maybe you've incurred so much debt that you need

251

a more aggressive approach to reducing it. Whatever the case, involve God. Again, when you agree to tithe at least ten percent of your income no matter what, God guarantees you will see a change in your financial circumstances (Malachi 3:10).

Please understand that if you are in a financial crisis at this moment, we can relate. If you remember, after remarrying, we were uncertain as to how to deal with merging our finances and our debts. Trust us when we say there was a sinkhole of debt between the two of us. Breaking these financial matters into smaller, three-month chunks made the process of paying them off more palatable and less overwhelming.

Financial matters also became very intense for us after Penny's back injury. Imagine our surprise and concern when she was forced to leave her well-paying job as a school district administrator. Once her sick leave ran dry and her paychecks stopped, we were confronted with the need to make radical cuts in our budget. While we were caught off guard by what happened, God wasn't a bit surprised. He knew what was coming and prepared us.

Several months prior to the accident (when we were both making a sizeable income) we discussed the possibility of buying a larger home that was closer to our school district. Of course, this purchase was discussed at several Mini-Marriage Retreats. The long commute to school was horrible and our house was relatively small. However, each time we looked into purchasing a new home, God closed the door. Confused at the time, we agreed that He was definitely leading us away from the purchase. We had no idea Penny would soon be off work and without a paycheck. Had we purchased a new home, we would have been strapped with a large mortgage payment that we never could have afforded on one salary.

This is just one example of the innumerable ways God has helped bring order to our finances. Never did we realize how setting goals in this category would so radically impact our lives and our ministry.

Home Goals

Any improvements or projects that need to be completed around the house are placed in this category. If you don't own a home, adapt this focus area to fit your circumstances or living conditions. Your goals might include organizing closets or rooms. Perhaps some deep cleaning needs to happen. Maybe you have the hope of owning a home and therefore, your goals are discussed and set based on that desire.

One of the stressors we commonly see contributing to conflict between spouses is a husband who feels nagged by his wife to do things around the house and a wife who gets frustrated because those things never get done. Penny and I have drastically different approaches to things that need to be done around the house. Penny jumps on it and I take my time. After the honeymoon wore off (of our remarriage) we started to have issues in this area. So, we created a shared quarterly *honey-do* list and made an agreement to help us deal with the differences in our timelines. If a project is placed on that list, we discuss who will be primarily responsible for completing it.

What I really love about this category is that Penny knows the tasks I have to complete will get done and I know I have three months to do them. She doesn't need to remind me. I admit that, at first, I took advantage of the ninety days and procrastinated until day eighty-nine to complete my tasks. I wasn't doing this to irritate Penny, but I soon realized that I was unnecessarily pushing her buttons by waiting until the last moment. Since then, I've changed my ways and learned the benefits of spacing my projects out over the three-month period.

Big Dreams and Possibilities

This category is just what it says. It took several retreats for us to realize we needed to regularly discuss and assess our hopes, dreams, and possibilities for our individual lives, as well as for our marriage. That's when we added this category into our retreats. Once we did, we grew increasingly excited about dreaming together with God. In the past, we had both experienced the agony of watching our fledgling dreams get sabotaged or put asunder by negative people, poor planning, or unfortunate circumstances. As a result, we are now very mindful to nurture each other's desires and to dream together as a couple.

Over the years since we started doing this, it's been an absolute joy to communicate our longings and explore all these possibilities with the God of the impossible. *Big Dreams and Possibilities* is most definitely an "all things considered" category. As our deepest desires are shared, we're careful to suspend judgment or criticism if we don't fully understand what's important to each other.

This category undeniably grants us the freedom to color far outside the lines or confines of "rational" thought. The book you are now holding is a result of writing down our dreams during several Mini-Marriage Retreats, as are our 40-Day Marriage Mission Trips and our ministry to couples in crisis.

The following pages contain a *Mini Marriage Retreat Goal Setting Worksheet* with sample goals listed in each category. For your convenience, there's a blank copy of this form located on pages 291-292.

Date: February, 2008   **Location:** Daytona Shores, FL

Mini-Marriage Retreat Sample Goals

Focus Area #1: **Spiritual**	Individual – memorize 3-4 verses of Scripture Together – meet one hour on Sunday nights for devotional time Family – share blessings and prayer requests more intentionally Church – engage in church makeover service project

Focus Area #2: **Relationships**	Together – date nights twice a month-alternate who plans the date Family – invite extended family over for dinner Friends – write personal notes to couples in our small group

Focus Area #3: **Health/Fitness**	Self – increase walking by .5 miles each day Spouse – integrate free-weight routine twice weekly Both – get complete physical from primary doctor

Focus Area #4: **Professional**	Self – attend two-day training in Atlanta Spouse – complete one professional growth unit toward credential Kids – help with school loan application

Focus Area #5: **Financial**	Give 15% tithe for at least two months Reduce monthly expenses by at least 10% Open Roth IRA for both of us

Focus Area #6: **Home**	Weed front flower bed and replant Repair back gate and section of fence Clean out storage shed and have garage sale Pray for protection from major expenses

Focus Area #7: **Big Dreams and Possibilities**	Self – publish a book about our mission trip experiences Spouse – attend one week video school Both – travel to Israel for study tour

Last Minute Trip Tips

There are a few other important tips we want to give you before you try your first Mini-Marriage Retreat. These things were developed over time with the hope of helping other couples implement this practice.

Agree to Disagree: Despite all the tools in our marriage tool belt, there have been times when we weren't in total agreement as to how we perceived a particular area of our marriage. You'll experience this as well. Expect to disagree, but take your differences of opinion to the Lord on the spot. As stated over and over in this book, ask God for the changes He wants to make in *your* heart and leave your spouse to Him. Remember to combine prayer with the Gradients of Agreement diagram as discussed in Chapter 5.

Divide and Conquer: Taking care of the logistics for a Mini-Marriage Retreat shouldn't fall on one spouse. This is a shared experience with shared responsibilities. On page 290 you'll find a *Know Before You Go* list that will help you prepare for retreats with the minimum amount of stress and/or obstacles. We now have our packing and prep time down to a minimum so we can maximize our time together. Also, remember that when you return from a retreat, divide and conquer the things awaiting you, such as laundry, picking up the kids, returning calls, unpacking, etc.

Heads Up: It took us a retreat or two to realize the Enemy was in direct opposition to our getaways. Expect an increase in spiritual warfare the week before you go away and the week after you return. Keep alert to Satan's desire to divide you and thwart your progress. Keep watch over each other as well.

Getting on the Same Page: We often use our retreats as an opportunity to choose a new book to read together. It's important that you approach this idea as a learning process. It will take you time to agree on preferred genres. Ask for God's help in choosing books and take turns making selections. We also recommend that, at first, you select shorter books. In time, you will learn about the kinds of books that "work" for both of you. We've included a brief list of some of our favorite books to read together on page 299. Ask your friends, pastors, or local Christian bookstore staff for their recommendations as well. Listed below, are some discussion prompts to get you "on the same page" with your spouse through reading and discussing Christian literature.

Discussion Prompts for Reading Books Together

- I can relate to this chapter because...
- One thing that spoke to my heart was...
- What do you think about...
- My favorite part of this book so far has been...
- One thing I want to apply from this chapter is...
- One of the things I appreciate about this author is...
- I want to know more about...
- I can identify with the author when he/she said...
- I would recommend this book to _____ because...
- A passage of Scripture that relates to this chapter is...
- I'm struggling with what we are reading because...

Talk to Other Couples: Is a Mini-Marriage Retreat the only way to assess your marriage or put margins of time and space around your relationship? Certainly not. You might come up with your own system or use parts of ours and combine those with other ideas you come across. Talk to other couples about how they assess their marriages and put margins in their lives. Spend time exchanging ideas. Remember that the key is *regularly* setting aside *quality* time for the purposes of assessing your relationship and its restoration. Perhaps you can partner with another couple and hold each other accountable to taking at least two Mini-Marriage Retreats this year.

Start Small, Pray Big: Take what we've suggested in this chapter one step at a time. Allow God to measure your marriage His way and embrace whatever means He uses to do so. He's planned out your course and has been longing for you to accept His invitation to an incredible journey. A large portion of that journey is taken through prayer. Our hope is that through each of your Mini-Marriage Retreats, you'll experience deeper intimacy in your marriage and your relationships with God. The moment you truly begin to tap into God's plan, perspective, and purpose for your marriage, you're in for the ride of your life. So, fasten your seatbelts and hang-on!

CHAPTER EXERCISES

Prayer to Manage Your Margins

God, You know the demanding pace of our lives. We need Your help to place margins of time and space around our marriage and family. Show us how to value stillness, reflection, conversation, and assessment. We acknowledge how important it is to measure our marriage the way You do, not as the world does. Make us sensitive to the passages in Your Word that demonstrate your *Law of Inversion* so we might learn Your ways. We ask for Your eternal priorities to become ours. Broaden our perspective so that we can see more than just our own needs, wants, and desires. Help us implement times of setting and assessing goals into all the important parts of our relationship. Bring other couples into our lives who share this same desire and help us partner with them. We open our hearts and minds to the ways You want to use the tools in this chapter to change our lives. In Jesus' name we pray. Amen.

Making Connections

As a practice run, take some time to set one sample goal together in each of the seven focus areas. Look over your calendar and budget to discuss how feasible Mini-Marriage Retreats would be and, if possible, set a date for your first one.

Scripture Reading

Read Nehemiah 12:27–47 and Nehemiah 13 before answering the questions on the next page.

Questions to Consider

1. What are some of your initial thoughts and reactions regarding the Mini-Marriage Retreat?

2. How might your marriage benefit from these retreats?

3. What is a feasible plan in terms of implementing something like a Mini-Marriage Retreat? In other words, is it conceivable to get away four times a year? Two? What are some of the specific or perceived obstacles to consider ahead of time?

4. After the dedication of Jerusalem's walls, why do you think Nehemiah returned to his service as the king's cupbearer, instead of staying in Jerusalem as governor?

5. What happened when Nehemiah later returned to Jerusalem to check on the people? How would you have felt if you were in his shoes and how would you have reacted?

6. Look back over your marriage timeline and identify the times when you took on too many responsibilities. How did that busy season impact your relationship? How might marriage margins have helped?

Although we wouldn't have said so at the time, hitting bottom was the best thing that ever happened to us. After fourteen years of marriage and three kids, we finally surrendered our plans to God and asked Him to re-blueprint our relationship. The process hasn't been easy, but we are fully aware of the fact that there have been nineteen divorces in our extended family and we aren't about to become number twenty!

Through our crisis, God has taught us how to eliminate all the parasites and distractions that were eating away at our intimacy. Because we finally made our individual relationships with Him the most important aspect of our lives, our marriage has remained on solid footing with a bright future ahead. We are committed to living by His principles and increasing our reliance on Him for continued healing. Our marriage is moving forward into a brand new covenant; one that is based on forgiveness, grace, and mercy.

Scott and Sylvia Harrelson
Danville, CA

Chapter 12 – Traveling Into New Territories

O f all the content we could have included in this closing chapter, our decision as to what made the final cut was a no-brainer. However, there was no shortage of options vying for control of the keyboard. For example, given the fact that we've spent eleven chapters avidly following on the heels of the Israelites as they rebuilt Jerusalem's wall, one option was to direct your attention to the project's astounding completion.

> *So the wall was completed on the twenty-fifth of Elul, in fifty-two days.*
>
> Nehemiah 6:15

Inconceivable! The wall around the city that had been lying in ruins for almost 150 years was repaired in less than two months. With society today driven by swift and favorable results, surely this noteworthy success merits our rapt attention…as does your progress, thus far, in restoring your marriage. If you've faithfully implemented the tools we've suggested throughout this book, then we're certain you've made significant growth in your relationship. However, unlike restoring Jerusalem, the restoration of your marriage will *never* end. Nehemiah and his hearty band of laborers eventually hung up their trowels and tool belts. But, if you follow suit, you'll find yourselves in a heap of trouble in nothing flat.

Until our last breath, we will declare that mending a marriage is not a one-time event, but an ongoing process you must nurture and cultivate each day for the rest of your lives. Reconciliation must become an integral thread in the fabric of your marriage, hemming in your identity as a couple; your "us" as husband and wife. Many couples make a very grave error when they incorrectly assume that once the disaster has passed and sufficient progress has been made in their marriage, they can stop applying the strategies that were so crucial to their restoration. Unknowingly and unintentionally, they sever the very things that seamed them back together. Please, don't follow that example.

There's *no* point at which you'll finish restoring your relationship. To this day, we admit that we still have things to work through and, by the sovereign hand of God, we always will. Some of this work is just part of the process He's using to transform us into Christ's image, and some of it comes from the poor choices we made in the past. Until the day we arrive at heaven's gates, God will not be finished restoring our marriage and we guarantee that as long as you are here, He won't be done with yours, either. So, if you ever look around and think you've arrived, we implore you: Take another look!

We also encourage you to reread the advice from the couples who've contributed their wisdom at the beginning of each chapter and those who were featured in various places throughout the book. Like you, somewhere in the courses of their crises, they decided to fight for their marriage. And, through a lot of hard work and God's grace, their marriages are making it. So, like us and every one of these couples, keep your tool belt strapped on tightly at all times. You're going to need it.

Another option jockeying for a prime position in this final chapter was the rich symbolism and historical significance of the ceremonies recorded in the latter half of Nehemiah, and the application of those to your marriage. Not only did our fearless leader carry out the registry of all the exiles who returned to Jerusalem, but he also called for a lavish and unprecedented time of confession and celebration. No sooner were the doors set into the gates than did Nehemiah appoint guards, gatekeepers, ministers, and singers to their respective places (Nehemiah 7:1). Then, in Chapters 8-12, we find the intricate details of an elaborate gathering which included the reading of God's Word, corporate confession and worship, and a public declaration of faith. Integrated into all of this was the customary Jewish celebration of the *Feast of Tabernacles*, which commemorated God's protection during the desert wanderings of their forefathers as they journeyed from Egypt to Canaan (Exodus 23). Just look at the way Nehemiah describes this grand affair:

From the days of Joshua son of Nun until that day, the Israelites had not celebrated it like this. And their joy was very great.

Nehemiah 8:17

It's hard to imagine what it must have been like to participate in festivities of this magnitude, the momentum of which had been building for centuries. When all was said and done, their celebration culminated in the dedication of Jerusalem's walls (Nehemiah 12).

Like the Israelites, the progress you've made in mending your marriage thus far is cause for much rejoicing. By all means, never hesitate to recall, acknowledge, and give thanks for what God has done. We commend you for courageously treading this challenging terrain. You've taken major strides on the road to healing and wholeness. Your family's spiritual legacy has been altered forever because of your journey. Retelling and reflecting on what has transpired in your relationship is extremely healthy, highly advocated, and downright biblical. We encourage you to pause often, ponder the rippling impact of deciding to save your marriage, and linger there…for a long, long time.

Of all the last words we could have offered you, however, the greatest temptation was to spend our sentences inspiring you with the unfathomable ways God is likely to use your testimony of reconciliation to help others. Gone are the days we incorrectly assumed that only people with perfect marriages served in marriage ministry. We're living proof of that misconception! We vividly remember sitting together at our first marriage and family conference secretly wondering, "God, You're not calling *us* into marriage ministry, are You? You've got to be kidding. *Us?*"

The people most equipped to work with couples in crisis are the couples who've been through the fire and risen from the ash heap with their hearts in full-blown pursuit of God; couples who are willing to show their scars and point people to the only One who can heal them. We never conceived that, one day, God would allow us to share our story of reconciliation from coast-to-coast. It's been a wild ride! As a matter of fact, as we pen this page, we're just days away from leaving on another 40-Day Marriage Mission Trip across the United States. Having embarked on several of these missions in years past, we know we're in store for a quite a journey. Each time we set foot outside our front door for forty days, we return home changed. We pray the same will be said for the people we'll meet and minister to along the way.

To be quite candid, however, advising you that God will lead you into marriage ministry is not our call to make. It's His, and we'd be foolish to intervene on such sacred turf. Historically, God is passionate about using the power of testimony to heal others. We're absolutely undone by the nature of His redemptive purposes in our pain. However, we also know there are dangers inherent in any attempt to use our words to foretell your future.

Having said that, if God has chosen to use your saved marriage story to serve others, we'll be the first people to wholeheartedly welcome you to the front lines of this noble work. Surely, we need more hands for the harvest! We'll be plowing, planting, sowing, and reaping right beside you in the effort to snatch back every inch of territory the Enemy has stolen. Oh, that this nation may overflow with a rich bounty of saved marriages to cast at our Savior's feet on that final Day!

So, with all these viable options for closing dialogue at our disposal, what admonitions did we decide to offer? Early on in the conception of this book, we knew that *anything* less than making one final shameless plea to launch you deeper into your relationship with God would be grossly negligent on our part.

We've entitled this chapter, "Traveling into New Territories" with the hope of enticing you into entering unprecedented realms of intimacy with God. Much more than encouraging you to strive for a breadth of spiritual accomplishments, it is the earnest cry of our hearts to inspire you to give God greater access to your lives than you've given Him up until now. It's the grand landscape of your soul that He longs to travel and, speaking from experience, when God moves in, He likes plenty of leg room.

Prone to Wander

No sooner had Nehemiah left Jerusalem and returned to the king's service, then did everything he'd labored for begin to unravel. It didn't take long for the people to become careless and apathetic toward their pursuit of God.

> *Before this, Eliashib the priest had been put in charge of the storerooms of the house of our God. He was closely associated with Tobiah, and he had provided him with a large room formerly used to store the grain offerings and incense and temple articles, and also the tithes of grain, new wine and oil prescribed for the Levites, singers and gatekeepers, as well as the contributions for the priests. But while all this was going on, I was not in Jerusalem, for in the thirty-second year of Artaxerxes king of Babylon I had returned to the king. Some time later I asked his permission and came back to Jerusalem. Here I learned about the evil thing Eliashib had done in providing Tobiah a room in the courts of the house of God. I was greatly displeased and threw all Tobiah's household goods out of the room. I gave orders to purify the rooms, and then I put back into them the equipment of the house of God, with the grain offerings and the incense. I also learned that the portions assigned to the Levites had not been given to them, and that all the Levites and singers responsible for the service had gone back to their own fields. So I rebuked the officials and asked them, "Why is the house of God neglected?"*

Nehemiah 13:4–11

Despite Nehemiah's exceptional leadership and the great lengths to which he worked to ensure the protection of Jerusalem…despite all the ceaseless striving, hard labor, new reforms, and a binding agreement to uphold the law that was sealed in public (Nehemiah 9:38), the Israelites made one critical error: they denied God *full* access to their hearts. Regardless of their humble confessions and an absolute resolve to remain faithful, they failed.

If you recall, Eliashib was one of the priests mentioned as a laborer at the Sheep Gate (Nehemiah 3:1). How ironic! No sooner did Nehemiah return to his service as the king's cupbearer, then did Eliashib give one of Israel's arch enemies access to a sacred room in the courts of God's Temple.

"We will not neglect the house of our God" (Nehemiah 10:39). If only the Israelites had lived out their words, instead of just reciting them. While the people accomplished an amazing feat in restoring the ruins of the city, they failed miserably in the reformation of their own hearts.

You see, the Israelites missed the boat on a major revelation: *the wall around Jerusalem was a symbol of the nation itself.* Consider that truth for a moment and let it sink in. Just as Nehemiah longed to repair Jerusalem's walls, God longed to revive His people…to shore up their foundation, to rebuild their broken places, and to restore them to an even greater glory than was evident in days of old. The walls of Jerusalem, which remained in such disrepair all those years, symbolized the disobedient state of the nation and yet, they never made that connection. This is a critical point to grasp regarding Israel and the labor at which they toiled. Unfortunately, this truth went right over their heads.

We mustn't be like the Israelites and miss the important lesson in all of this. Throughout many places in the Word, God used a wall to serve as a symbol of His people. Psalms, Isaiah, Ezekiel, and Song of Solomon all include references of this sort. While the Israelites may have succeeded in accomplishing a monumental work, they missed out on realizing the true measure of God's monumental love for them.

The heart of His chosen people had been invaded by the things of the world and, as a result, she was defenseless. Just as other nations laid siege to Jerusalem, battered down her walls, burned her gates, and invaded her territory, disobedience had done the same thing to the people. Sin had ravaged their hearts for generations and, as a result, their relationship with God lay crumbled. When all was said and done, only ruins remained. However, God had a plan to restore the nation…and His people.

Staying True to Form

> This is what he showed me: The Lord was standing by a wall that had been built true to plumb, with a plumb line in his hand. And the LORD asked me, "What do you see, Amos?" "A plumb line," I replied. Then the Lord said, "Look, I am setting a plumb line among my people Israel; I will spare them no longer."
>
> Amos 7:7–8

Biblical references to a *plumb line* almost always symbolized how righteous or upright the people were living (or not living) according to God's Word. A plumb line signified the standard by which God would judge His people, and the mention of it let them know that enough was enough: judgment was coming. While God's people were originally created *true to plumb*, when tests and trials arose, they did not remain upright. A righteous and just God simply could not sit idly by and allow their disobedience to continue.

During the reconstruction of Jerusalem's walls, Nehemiah and the other laborers would have used a plumb line: a simple tool consisting of a cord at the end of which a stone or weight was suspended, pointing directly to the earth's center of gravity. Although we don't see this tool specifically mentioned in the book of Nehemiah, we can safely assume it was used to ensure that, as the restoration progressed, the walls were being built true to plumb.

We have the benefit of hindsight and history and are wise to learn many valuable lessons from the mistakes the Israelites made. Unfortunately, a passing glance at our nation today proves that many people still haven't learned these lessons. Sadly, the human heart—something so precious to God—is treated like nothing more than a cheap bargaining chip. As a nation, we're quick to turn what is sacred into something profane. Between round-the-clock assaults from mass media, technological advances, and Internet offerings at our fingertips, the pursuit of earthly pleasures over kingdom purposes beckons daily at our heart's door.

The sobering reality is that every one of us, despite the high morals to which we may hold, is just one click away from desecrating God's dwelling place. That being the case, allow us to be quite bold here. If you aren't spending what fleeting time you have left on earth intentionally and reverently seeking after God, somewhere down the road you'll find yourself in crisis all over again. No sooner will you close the last page of this book than will it, and your marriage, sit on a shelf collecting dust. If you don't seek to fill every square inch of your heart with more of God, it *will* get filled with other things.

Like the ancient Israelites, we need a plumb line, and we have one in Jesus Christ. Through His death, Jesus humbly held the bar by which we must measure our spiritual lives and marriages. In several respects, Nehemiah and many other prophets, saints, apostles, martyrs, and disciples were forerunners of the plumb line who was to come. Like Christ, these forerunners chose to exercise humility over power and to forgive instead of fight. Like Christ, their attitudes and actions went against the grain of the world. The manner by which they stayed true to plumb was so unfathomable that, more often than not, they were persecuted for rubbing the world the wrong way, especially when it came to relationships. Take a look at just a few examples of these courageous forerunners found in the pages of God's Word:

- Abraham bound his son and his hopes to the altar of sacrifice.
- David had Saul at the end of his spear, yet refused to take revenge.
- Ruth remained by her mother-in-law's side, instead of returning to her homeland.
- Hannah gave birth after years of barrenness, and then gave her son back to God.
- Joseph forgave his jealous brothers, despite their attempt to kill him.
- Esther risked her life to save a city from annihilation.
- Hosea reconciled with his wife, even though she'd sold herself for sex.

If you took the time to trace the favorable fall-out from the decisions of just those seven individuals, you'd discover that they drastically altered the course of human history. There are

272

many more people—past and present—to add to that list as well. What all these heroes of our faith have in common is that they learned to live under God's *Law of Inversion* in *every* aspect of their lives, especially where relationships were concerned. They understood that in order to be great, they must become the least, and that to have true love, they must give love away.

Perhaps what is just as extraordinary as living plumb to God's principles is the fact that sheer love and devotion was the guiding force behind their choices. You won't find a single verse in the Bible where God stood there, twisting anyone's arm.

As we've seen throughout *Marriage on the Mend*, our beloved, Nehemiah, made those same kinds of *inverted* choices. Please allow us one more opportunity to extract a few final principles from our favorite prophet; truths so subtle and counter-culture that, to be quite honest, they're easily overlooked and tempting to avoid. As a matter of fact, it wasn't until we engaged in a much more active and intentional approach to our relationships with God that we began to scratch past the surface of the three empowering *plumb line principles* we're about to unpack. Grasping onto the truths these principles represent will undeniably hold you and your marriage true to God's original design. Before we begin, it's worth noting that, unlike the previous lessons we've extracted from this prophet, these principles are revealed, not through what Nehemiah did, but through what he *didn't* do.

Plumb Line Principle 1: Less-is-More

Throughout the course of his life, Nehemiah *never* chose opportunism over service. His priority was to be a humble servant; first to God, then to his fellow man. He was a servant leader and he lived out that characteristic in various forms. For example, unlike other political figures, instead of demanding the food rightfully allotted to him, his main concern was making sure others had what they needed. Nehemiah wasn't worried about feeding his stomach, or his ego.

During his tenure as governor, he also chose not to acquire any land. Having a servant's heart for God and His people was the overriding principle that set Nehemiah's priorities in order. Any possessions he may have acquired were never hoarded. Instead, research indicates that Nehemiah regularly entertained a variety of guests at his own expense. And, although he had every right to draw a salary, Nehemiah chose not to do so (Nehemiah 5:14–19).

Another example of this *less-is-more* lifestyle is that Nehemiah never neglected the poor or powerless. As soon as he became aware of the abuse occurring amongst the laborers by their lenders, he stopped the project mid-stream to put an end to this oppression. He made certain the workers wouldn't be abused by those who were charging interest on loans and enslaving the children as collateral (Nehemiah 5).

What is the bottom line in all of this? Over and over again, Nehemiah put *God's* priorities before His own. Like Jesus, Nehemiah was a selfless servant who was not interested in amassing possessions or acquiring status. We are called to do the same.

Plumb Line Principle 2: No Compromise

As far as Nehemiah was concerned, there was *no* justification for disregarding of God's Word. For example, as a layman, the law did not permit Nehemiah to enter the Temple. So, when his enemies encouraged him to run there for cover, he wasn't about to take a cowardly turn against God's commands. Even with his life at stake, Nehemiah didn't take shortcuts or transgress against the statutes in God's Word (Nehemiah 6:11).

Nehemiah was also committed to keeping the regulations that God set down as sacred. He never neglected the importance of worship (Nehemiah 12:40–43), disregarded the sanctity of the Sabbath (Nehemiah 13:19–22), or shrugged off his duties in God's house (Nehemiah 10:28–39).

In spite of everything he faced, Nehemiah didn't compromise his integrity because he revered God and highly regarded His history with mankind. The entire ninth chapter of Nehemiah includes a record of God's miracles, judgments, and deliverance of the Jews from Egyptian rule. Nehemiah knew how important it was to remember God's faithfulness in the past, as well as His promise to guide the future.

Whether he was dealing with peasants or kings, Nehemiah *consistently* led a life of *no compromise*. If you remember, he had asked King Artaxerxes for permission to leave his service as the King's cupbearer in order to help rally the people to restore the city. When the project was complete, however, Nehemiah left Jerusalem and humbly returned to the King's court, just as he'd promised (Nehemiah 13:6). Nehemiah was a man of his word, something that, unfortunately, is quite rare today.

God longs for His people to *"become blameless and pure, children of God without fault in a crooked and depraved generation"* (Philippians 2:15).

Plumb Line Principle 3: No Confidence in the Flesh

Nehemiah didn't rely on his own strength to overcome his enemies. He consistently looked to God to be his strength and his confidence. Despite repeated assaults, ridicule, scorn, and threats, he never conceded to the opposition. Nehemiah remained tenacious and persevered through every obstacle he encountered. When his enemies threatened to stop forward progress, Nehemiah refused to give ear to their accusations. During the reconstruction, he didn't retaliate against his opponents, but relied on God to settle every dispute and fight every battle on his behalf. Nehemiah wasn't concerned about how weak he appeared to those around him and he wasn't too proud to ask for help. Nehemiah was secure in his identity as God's very own (Nehemiah 4:6; 19–21; 6:16).

In a tangible way, Nehemiah's leadership was characterized by his willingness to follow. Although Nehemiah was known for being a skillful administrator, he didn't have to call the shots all the time. Like the apostle Paul, Nehemiah knew that in his weakness, God's power would be manifested (Nehemiah 12:31–39).

In addition to all these examples of God's strength exhibited in Nehemiah's weakness, Nehemiah never sought the accolades of others. Instead, his greatest concern was to be remembered as a man of God. If a record was to be kept of Nehemiah's good deeds, he wanted it noted in *God's* register, not in the annals of men (Nehemiah 13:14, 22, 31).

The reason we explain these three plumb line principles is to stress their powerful application to your marriage. All of these intentional choices—so very characteristic of Jesus, Nehemiah, and many others in the Bible—must constitute the *culture* of your marriage…who you are as one flesh. The inverted lifestyle, refusing to compromise in any area of your life, and fully relying on God for all things must serve as the plumb line for keeping you focused on your vertical relationship with Him throughout your journey together as husband and wife. Choosing kingdom priorities over earthly pursuits automatically grants you greater access to more intense pleasure and intimacy than you could ever conceive. As if that isn't enough, it's also an incredibly purposeful way to live the rest of your lives for God!

The Momentum to Turn the Tide

Penny and I only realized the true power of these principles when we tried them out for ourselves. Unbeknownst to either of us at the time, we'd both crashed and burned during the years following our divorce. Eventually, we found ourselves in desperate straits; a place on the journey we referred to in an earlier chapter as "the bottom of the bottom." Living on opposite coasts of the United States at the time, we were broken and humbled before God; finally acknowledging that we'd made huge messes of our lives.

For me, the surrender came when I finally admitted I'd been angry at God for the way Penny and I split up. Although I would never admit it at the time, for years I secretly blamed Him for our divorce. After finally confessing my anger, I immediately asked for His forgiveness. I let go of everything I'd been harboring and all the things of earth upon which I'd been building my life. Several weeks later, I darkened the doorway of a church; something I hadn't done in years. Then, and only then, did God allow Penny to come back into my life.

I'll never forget the day her letter arrived. I was coming home from my job as a real estate agent. Grabbing a stack of letters and bills from the mailbox, I hurried up the front steps and put the key into the lock on the front door. When I looked down at the envelope on top of the pile, my jaw dropped. My heart sank down to my knees…and came back up. I stumbled inside the house, placed the envelope on my desk, and stared at it for a long time.

"Lord, should I open it…or not?"

It had been over a decade since I'd seen or heard from Penny. With a unique mixture of shock and awe, I opened the envelope. Inside was a letter that read…

Dear Clint,   February 18, 2002

I have no idea if this letter will even reach you. I pray that it will. As a matter of fact, my intent to contact you has been bathed in prayer for almost a year. Now that I think I finally have your latest address, there's no excuse for me to hesitate any longer, except for my own fears as to how you might react, or that you will not respond. Honestly, I don't really expect anything in return from you, unless you feel led to do so. My hope is that I would at least know that you received this and read it.

My intent in writing this is to bring healing to my life and hopefully yours. It is not to bring you pain or open old wounds. As I've been actively seeking the Lord's will for my life over the last three years, one thing has been clear. He has shown me ways in which I clearly left my relationship with you unresolved. He has shown me that I made some serious mistakes with huge consequences. He has directed me to apologize to you and to ask your forgiveness. Let me start with the last.

Continued on the next page…

278

I know that I would be crazy to think that a letter 10+ years after the fact would be adequate in admitting my wrongdoing. I know that it is not. Actually, I would prefer talking with you by phone or face-to-face because I believe that you deserve that. However, I figured I'd start with a letter. If God allows this to move toward a conversation down the road, I'm game if you are.

I am very sorry for my part in the breakdown of our marriage and I do ask for your forgiveness. As I have grown older (and hopefully wiser), I have certainly seen more clearly the ways in which I contributed to our divorce. Again, mere words fail, but perhaps we'll have the opportunity to try and get it right down the road.

I also want to confess that when I was first urged to contact you, about a year ago, it was because I was dating a man and had thoughts of a future marriage, family, etc. I realized that in order to know God's will and whether or not He would even approve of a marriage, I needed to go back to heal some things from our marriage and truly seek out His answers. We are no longer dating, however, I decided that a relationship with another person is not the catalyst I should be using to make me finally contact you. I should contact you simply because it's the right thing to do, it would please the Lord, and I want my relationship with Him to be more intimate. And so, now is the right time.

Continued on the next page…

279

> I have been on my own for several years now. Solitude has drawn me to a relationship with Christ that I never thought possible. I am continually amazed by His grace and unconditional love for me, despite my many mistakes. Enclosed is a CD that might give you a better glimpse into where I am on this journey called life.
>
> I have no doubt that you have been successful at whatever you have put your mind to. You were always very determined. I do think of you often and wonder what you are up to. It's hard to believe this much time has passed and how far apart we are. It is my hope and prayer that this letter might begin to bridge the gap between us and that God will soften your heart to consider my words.
>
> Clint, please pray about this. Know that I will continue praying long after this letter leaves my hands and is placed into His…and ultimately, yours.
>
> Penny

While I (Penny) long to author a hundred books before I die, the most important thing I could ever write has already been written in that letter. God took the very thing that I had hoped would bring *closure* to the past and used it to bust our future wide open.

It took eleven years and some agonizing lessons in the school of hard knocks, but when the time was right and we had made the decision to truly put Him first in our individual lives, God drew in a big, deep breath and blew a whirlwind of new life into a dead marriage. We share that letter with you (in its entirety) to illustrate and reiterate that *this* is the God of reconciliation we worship and serve. This is *our* God! A God of healing and redemption! *This is our God!* A God who plucks sinners from the misery they've made of their lives, presses them against His bosom, and makes them whole.

Like our marriage, your reconciliation is now part of the groundswell that will turn the tide of shattered relationships and transform the face of our nation from a dismal frown into one of radiant countenance! Make no mistake. Every reconciled marriage delivers yet another death-blow deep into the gut of evil.

Dear friend, while the world wags its tail in wait for some cutting edge politician to heal the ills plaguing this nation, God has already given us the catalyst for true change through Jesus Christ. He is looking for people who want to be purified for a sacred purpose and who will *voluntarily* live a less-is-more lifestyle out of gratitude and devotion to Him. At this very moment, God is searching the earth for people who are without compromise; who place no confidence in their own flesh, but who will consciously choose to walk out their faith in humble acts of profound obedience. Can you imagine what would happen in our world today if *everyone* caught on?

A Change of Season

We firmly believe God is just waiting to cut loose with an unprecedented supernatural revival on all fronts and that the threatening tide of divorce will dramatically turn back through forgiveness and reconciliation; one couple at a time. Over and over again, the Bible proves that the grandeur of God is called forth and released when we walk counter-intuitive to the flesh and, instead, step in full stride with the Spirit. Up until this very moment, we've never publicly declared what we're about to disclose, but here goes.

During our very first 40-Day Marriage Mission Trip in the fall of 2006, God specifically spoke to us about a revival of marriage and family across our nation. It all started in a living room in Ypsilanti, Michigan.

We were staying in the home of our dear friends, Ben and Jennifer. On one particular evening, the four of us decided to spend some time talking and praying about our shared passion for marriage and family ministry. Just prior to leaving for this mission, we'd also been asked by our ministry partners, Eric and Jennifer Garcia (founders of the *Association of Marriage and Family Ministries*), to pray for one month over the following verse:

> *If my people, who are called by my name, will humble themselves and pray and seek my face and turn from their wicked ways, then will I hear from heaven and will forgive their sin and will heal their land.*

> 2 Chronicles 7:14

At the end of that month, Eric and Jennifer wanted us to report what we sensed God was saying about restoring our nation through marriage and family ministries.

As Clint prayed aloud in Ben and Jennifer's living room, the Holy Spirit dropped something sacred into my heart: *"There will be a turning of a Fifth Season...a supernatural season of the Holy Spirit's revival upon marriages and families across this nation."*

Fast forward a few years and a couple more 40-Day Marriage Mission Trips and the turning of a supernatural *Fifth Season* is now firmly lodged in our hearts. We believe that a

Fifth Season—a season absolutely impossible in the natural realm—will be ushered in by, *"the God who gives life to the dead and calls things that are not as though they were"* (Romans 4:17). The God who can turn a shameful past into a hopeful future. The God who can breathe brand new life into a very dead marriage.

The decision to reconcile and restore our marriage, your marriage, and the marriages of all the other couples you've met through the pages of this book has created a major surge in the momentum to usher the Fifth Season into full manifestation. Whenever you are tempted to toss in the towel on your relationship (and you will be tempted) you must remember the eternal significance of saving your marriage, and unequivocally refuse to give up or give in.

In our letter to you at the beginning of this book, we posed the question: *What if?* And now, at the conclusion of this final chapter, we ask the very same question.

What if together, as husband and wife, you decided to voluntarily live the *less-is-more lifestyle*? What if you committed to building a marriage and family of *no compromise*? And, what if you put *no confidence in the flesh* but, instead, fixed all your hope in the power of the Holy Spirit?

Perhaps of all the qualities we've grown to love about our man, Nehemiah, and what endears him to our hearts the most is this: *he never left well enough alone*. More than any one thing we could possibly speak into your life, we beg you: *Don't leave well enough alone…in your marriage…in your family…or in your relationship with God.*

As you turn the last page of this book, we pray that you now possess a more insatiable hunger for God than when you opened the first.

Burst into songs of joy together, you ruins of Jerusalem, for the LORD has comforted his people, he has redeemed Jerusalem. The LORD will lay bare his holy arm in the sight of all the nations, and all the ends of the earth will see the salvation of our God.

Isaiah 52:9–10

CHAPTER EXERCISES

Prayer to Travel into New Territories

Gracious God, we worship You. Only You can save our marriage. Only You can make us whole and complete. We want more of You, God. Increase our appetite for Your Word. Place a greater desire for Your truth in both of our hearts. We give You full access to our hearts, our marriage, and our family. Teach us how to live a less-is-more lifestyle. Holy Spirit, we ask You to convict our hearts when we're tempted to compromise or take shortcuts. We confess our weaknesses and draw upon Your strength now as we continue on in this journey called marriage. We know that our relationship will never be fully restored until we get to heaven, but teach us how to live as one flesh in every area of our lives. May You allow us to boldly step forward into new territories of intimacy and faith with You all the days of our lives together. In Jesus' name we pray. Amen.

Making Connections

Together, spend some time in God's Word and locate at least five other people who exhibit the *plumb line principles* discussed in this chapter. Then, trace the favorable fall-out from their counter-culture decisions and the impact of those decisions on history.

In addition, lay out the blank section of your marriage timeline and spend some moments together asking God to have His way with what is to come. Offer God the future of your marriage and give Him permission to begin writing a whole new chapter in your lives—one that is deeply rooted in Jesus Christ!

Questions to Consider

1. In your own words, explain the truth in the following statement from this chapter: "The wall of Jerusalem was a symbol of the nation itself."

2. Which of the three *plumb line principles* spoke to your heart the most: *the less-is-more* lifestyle, living a life of *no compromise*, or placing *no confidence in the flesh*? Explain your answer.

3. As you continue to deepen and move forward in your marriage, which tools from this book do you need to keep most handy at all times?

4. How can you apply the following statement to your marriage right now? "Don't leave well enough alone."

References and Research Sources

1. KDKA News, *Maryland Father Charged in Murder of Three Kids,* Pittsburg, Pennsylvania. April, 2008. www.kdka.com/national/dad.kills.kids.2.688544.html.

2. The Barna Group, Ventura, CA, *New Marriage and Divorce Statistics Released,* March, 2008. www.barna.org.

3. McGee, J. Vernon, *Thru the Bible, Volume II,* Thomas Nelson, 1982, p. 510.

4. Warren, Rick, *The Purpose Driven Life,* Zondervan, 2002.

5. Begay Gerri, *Nowhere to Turn, but Up,* Indian Life, July-August, 1990.

6. Gunter, Sylvia, *Prayer Essentials for Living in His Presence—Volume 1,* The Father's Business, 2000, p. 153.

7. Gordon, Lori H., *PAIRS International, Inc.*—Practical Application of Intimate Relationship Skills, Weston, FL. www.pairs.com.

8. Hirst, K. Kris, *Why Do Conquering Civilizations Rebuild in the Same Place?* About.com www.archaeology.about.com/od/questionoftheweek/qt/buried_sites2.htm.

9. McGee, J. Vernon, *The Gospel in the Gates of Jerusalem,* Thru the Bible Radio Network, p. 10.

10. Adeney, Walter, F., *Ezra, Nehemiah, and Esther,* Hodder and Stoughton Publishers, London, 1906, p. 230.

11. Stanley, Charles, *Living in the Power of the Holy Spirit,* Thomas Nelson, 2005, pp. 96-97.

12. Harris, Micki Ann, *Teaching Notes on Lessons from the Life of Nehemiah,* 1999.

13. Bragg, Penny A., *The Path of Most Resistance—A True Story of Reconciliation and Hope,* Inverse Ministries, 2004.

14. Bragg, Clint and Penny, *Dance Lessons—A Weekly Devotional Guide for Couples,* Inverse Ministries, 2004.

15. McGee, J. Vernon, *Thru the Bible, Volume II,* Thomas Nelson, 1982, pp. 520-521.

Know Before You Go!

Pray before, during, and after your Mini-Marriage Retreat. Realize that the Enemy is opposed to this idea!

Ask God to help you select a location. Decide which of you will be responsible for making the arrangements.

Determine your budget ahead of time.

Secure your reservations.

Print out directions to alleviate getting lost or wasting time.

Get familiar with what's nearby (restaurants, movie theaters, mini-marts) and what isn't nearby. Plan accordingly.

Pack snacks and munchies ahead of time to save money.

Discuss your expectations for the retreat beforehand.

Discuss timelines (when you will leave, return, pick-up the kids, etc.).

Secure child and/or pet care. (To save money, consider *house swaps*, *child swaps*, and *pet swaps* with other couples who also want to take a Mini-Marriage Retreat.)

Discuss possible things to do together on the retreat.

Leave your excess baggage at home (work, e-mail, cell phones).

Date: _____   Location: _____

Mini-Marriage Retreat Goal Setting Worksheet

Focus Area #1: _____ _____	....

Focus Area #2: _____ _____	....

Focus Area #3: _____ _____	....

Focus Area #4:
_____
_____
....
....
....
....

Focus Area #5:
_____
_____
....
....
....
....

Focus Area #6:
_____
_____
....
....
....
....

Focus Area #7:
_____
_____
....
....
....
....

Additional Resources

General Marriage and Family

Association of Marriage and Family Ministries (AMFM)
www.amfmonline.com
AMFM is an extensive network of grassroots ministries that equip pastors and leaders with comprehensive marriage and family tools and resources.

Family Friendly Partners Network
www.familyfriendlypn.com
Family Friendly Partners Network trains and equips churches to partner with homes in order to pass on faith in Jesus Christ to the third and fourth generations.

Focus on the Family
www.focusonthefamily.com
Focus on the Family is dedicated to reaching people with the Gospel of Jesus Christ by nurturing and defending the institution of the family and promoting biblical truth.

Healthy Christian Marriages
www.HealthyChristianMarriages.com
Healthy Christian Marriages is a group of New England-based pastors and leaders who promote healthy Christian marriages through mentoring, retreats, and special events.

Marriage Co-Mission
www.marriagecomission.com
Marriage Co-Mission supports the marriage movement in America by strengthening teamwork and pooling resources.

Marriage Missions International
www.marriagemissions.com
Marriage Missions International exists to inspire, encourage, and equip those who are married and those preparing for marriage by providing practical, biblical resources.

Visionary Parenting
www.visionaryparenting.com
Visionary Parenting is dedicated to helping parents and churches catch a biblical vision for the purpose of the family.

Reconciliation and Restoration

Broken Heart on Hold
www.brokenheartonhold.com
Broken Heart on Hold provides resources and support to women who are separated.

Family Dynamics
www.familydynamics.net
Family Dynamics helps couples, churches, and other organizations take proactive steps to prevent marriages from reaching a state of distress, and also reaches out to couples and families in crisis.

Hope & Healing Ministries
www.hopeandhealing.us
Hope and Healing is a ministry devoted to helping couples who have experienced the heartache of adultery.

International Center for Reconciling God's Way
www.reconcilingGodsway.org
Reconciling God's Way is a first response ministry that offers effective and affordable reconciliation tools and resources that work, even with an unwilling spouse.

Inverse Ministries, Inc.
www.inverseministries.org
Inverse Ministries is a husband and wife team who travel across the nation as marriage missionaries, bringing God's message of hope and reconciliation to hurting couples.

Journey to Wholeness in Christ
www.christanglican.com
Journey to Wholeness in Christ is a conference that allows attendees to experience the deep healing power of the Holy Spirit through biblically-based teaching, worship, personal testimony, and the individual ministry of the Journey Prayer Team.

Mountain Haven Marriage and Family Reconciliation Ministry
www.mountainhavenmarriageministry.com
Mountain Haven is a retreat center specializing in reconciliation.

National Institute of Marriage
www.nationalmarriage.com
National Institute of Marriage offers marriage intensives for couples in crisis.

Saved Marriage Network
www.SavedMarriageNetwork.com
Saved Marriage Network provides access to a wealth of marriage-saving resources.

Other Marriage and Family Resources

Creative Connections Ministry
www.creativeconnectionsministry.com
Creative Connections is dedicated to helping blended families.

Changing Families
www.ChangingFamilies.com
Changing Families specializes in supporting single-parents and blended families.

Faith and True Ministries
www.faithfulandtrueministries.com
www.southpointbaptist.org/psalm51.htm
Faithful and True is a recovery ministry for individuals and couples who struggle with sexual addiction.

Focus on Purpose
www.focusonpurpose.com
Focus on Purpose provides coaching for couples who want to work together to find their life-purpose.

Grace and Truth Relationship Education
www.graceandtruthrelationship.com
Grace and Truth Relationship Education offers classes, coaching and consultation services for a variety of marriage and family issues.

Hope Marriage Ministries
www.hopemarriageministries.org
Hope Marriage Ministry is committed to sharing God's precepts for marriage and family relationships.

InStep Ministries
www.instepministries.com
InStep Ministries provides biblical support and counsel to single, divorced and remarried individuals, their families, and the churches that minister to them.

Stubborn Pursuits Ministries
www.stubbornpursuits.com
Stubborn Pursuits is a ministry that offers marriage coaching, multiple assessment tools, training, and relationship education.

Walk and Talk
www.walkandtalk.org
Walk and Talk offers Christian counseling and a wide variety of interactive communication workshops.

Winshape Retreat Center
www.winshape.org
Winshape offers a variety of marriage strengthening programs in a beautiful country setting.

Online Bible Study Aids

Back to the Bible
www.backtothebible.com
Back to the Bible provides access to classic devotionals and other Bible study helps.

Bible.com
www.bible.com
Bible.com has an extensive collection of resources and is a great jumping-off point for other websites.

Bible Gateway
www.biblegateway.com
Bible Gateway is a free service for reading and researching Scripture in the language or translation of your choice.

Crosswalk
www.crosswalk.com
Crosswalk contains daily devotional resources, Bible study tools, Christian music reviews, and much more.

Into Thy Word
www.intothyword.org
Into Thy Word provides Christians with effective tools and means to better understand and apply God's Word.

International House of Prayer
www.ihop.org
The *International House of Prayer* site contains a wealth of downloadable audio and video podcasts.

Recommended Daily Devotionals

At His Feet, Chris Tiegreen (Tyndale, 2003).
Devotions for Men, Stuart Briscoe (Tyndale, 2000).
Devotions for Women, Jill Briscoe (Tyndale, 2000).
My Utmost for His Highest, Oswald Chambers (Discovery House, multiple versions available).
Streams in the Desert, L. Cowman (Zondervan, multiple versions available).
This Day with the Master, Dennis F. Kinlaw (Zondervan, 2002).

Books to Read Together

Can My Marriage Be Saved? Mae and Erika Chambers (Pass-it-On Publications, 2008).
Dance Lessons—A Weekly Devotional Guide for Couples, Clint and Penny Bragg (Bragg, 2004).
Dream Releasers, Wayne Cordeiro (Regal, 2002).
Living in the Power of the Holy Spirit, Charles Stanley (Thomas Nelson, 2005).
The Dream Giver, Bruce Wilkinson (Multnomah, 2003).
The Fasting Key, Mark Nysewander (Servant Publications, 2003).
The Love Dare, Stephen and Alex Kendrick (B and H Publishing, 2008).
The Purpose-Driven Life, Rick Warren (Zondervan, 2002).
Unfaithful—Hope and Healing After Infidelity, Gary and Mona Shriver (Cook, 2009).
Yes, Your Marriage Can be Saved, Joe and Michelle Williams (Focus on the Family, 2007).

Acknowledgments

Heartfelt Gratitude to...

The courageous couples who openly shared their marriage stories with us.

The warriors of intercession who bowed before the Father on our behalf during the writing of this book and our 40-Day Marriage Mission Trips.

Our monthly financial supporters who continue to give to our service as marriage missionaries, despite what the economy has to say about it.

The gifted individuals who took time away from their own projects to assist us during the editing process: Jason and Micah Burke, Kathy Coryell, Micki Ann Harris, Annie Jones, Joe Nassise, Sue Senadenos, Mona Shriver, and Michelle Williams.

Eric and Jennifer Garcia and the AMFM family who invite us to serve alongside them in ministry and open door after door for us with profound grace.

Dale and Colleen Goncalves who mentor us and serve as our wise sounding board.

Micki Ann Harris whose tender encouragement, biblical wisdom, and fervent prayer brought this baby to full-term.

Dr. Dale Hummel who reviewed our manuscript for biblical accuracy and provided us with helpful feedback.

Dawn Hutton Nassise who fearlessly jumped in during the final phase and generously donated her editing skills to us.

Annie Jones whose gifted and effortless way with words never fails to make perfect sense out of what we're trying to say.

Dr. Johnathan Mun who made our manuscript look delicious and his beloved wife, Penny, who covered every stage of this book in prayer.

Clifford F. Asher whose keen genius helped to make our dream a reality, the second time around.

Our loving families who continue to sacrifice our presence in California so that marriages and families across the nation can find healing.

Inverse Ministries, Inc.
40-Day Marriage Mission Trips

> **Our Purpose:**
> To reconcile broken marriages
> across the nation, reclaiming
> the territory of marriage
> and family for God!

Clint and Penny Bragg are available to...

- Share their testimony of reconciliation
- Teach seminars to restore and strengthen marriages
- Train ministry leaders to implement a ministry of reconciliation

www.inverseministries.org

Inverse Ministries is a non-profit corporation. We raise all of our support through tax-deductable donations so there is no financial burden on the churches or families to whom we minister.